HOW TO MAKE
A FORTUNE
IN SELF-PUBLISHING

HOW TO MAKE
A FORTUNE
IN SELF-PUBLISHING

James E. Neal, Jr.

Publishing Since 1978

HOW TO MAKE
A FORTUNE
IN SELF-PUBLISHING

Neal Publications, Inc.
127 W. Indiana Avenue
P.O. Box 451
Perrysburg, Ohio 43552-0451

ISBN 1-882423-29-1
SAN 240-8198
Library of Congress Catalog Card Number 93-92808

Table of Contents

Foreword

I am writing this book in response to numerous inquiries concerning self-publishing.

Neal Publications was founded as a sideline business in the basement of my home. Our first office was located on a card table. Since the early years, I have written five books including this one. We have sold several hundred thousand copies of various self-help titles.

Successful self-publishing is not an ego trip. Profits from book publishing have helped me put two children through college including medical school, purchase a second home, build an executive house and develop a sizeable investment portfolio. Our Company's growth has enabled us to purchase a splendid building in a modern business center.

My marketing background has heavily influenced the contents of this book. I believe that success in self-publishing is 5% writing and 95% selling.

This book is not a theoretical approach to self-publishing. Instead, it concentrates on running a self-publishing business based on fifteen years of solid experience.

I hope that our experiences will prove to be valuable to others who are contemplating a similar venture.

"Of making many books there is no end"

Ecclesiastes Chapter xii, Verse 12

I
Why Self-Publishing Is a Winner

Book publishing is a fascinating business. Attempting to get a book published, however, is a risky and often frustrating experience. It is very discouraging to submit numerous query letters and manuscripts to publishers and receive rejection letter after rejection letter.

Even if a book is published, its future remains uncertain. Every year, about 50,000 new titles are published in the United States. After a year or two, the number of new titles remaining in active print is greatly reduced.

A walk through any bookstore will usually find bargain tables filled with close out books with a printed price of $19.95 selling for as low as $1.00.

Self-publishing allows you to have complete control over the success of your venture. Compared to other businesses, self-publishing offers the following advantages:

1. low start-up costs
2. ability to operate out of your home
3. easy to relocate
4. ideally suited as a part-time venture
5. potential for full-time employment
6. national and international customer base
7. low labor costs
8. strongly compatible with office technology
9. special mailing rates provided by Congress
10. no professional license or education required

11. growth potential in related areas
12. nonperishable product

One of the great benefits of self-publishing is that it can be operated as a sideline venture. With more and more individuals facing growing job uncertainties, self-publishing can be a strong safety net. Once the business is in place, the opportunities for full-time involvement and increased profitability are tremendous.

Self-publishing can be a powerful springboard to even broader career opportunities. A successful self-publisher may find a bright future in conducting seminars and other teaching positions. Many authors have become sought after speakers.

You can publish a book in a reasonable quantity for about $3,500, including professional typesetting and quality printing but not including office equipment. For about $7,500, you can publish a softcover perfect-bound book and equip your office.

Keep in mind that you cannot accomplish business success without hard work and taking a risk. Many individuals desire to be authors but not publishers. After all, authors are considered to be intellectual, authoritative and sophisticated. Many would-be authors are really looking for an ego trip.

Executives, for example, love to be introduced as the author of _____. Never mind that the book has been sold to only a few relatives and close associates.

To be a successful self-publisher, you need to have strong confidence in yourself. Our first order to a printer was for 500 books. The printer said that the book would never sell. We have since sold several hundred thousand copies of the book that "would never sell."

Writing, publishing and selling a book is a time-consuming and serious business. You will probably begin by performing the services of a CEO, secretary, order taker, shipping clerk, bookkeeper and custodian. If you possess the enthusiasm, determination and the entrepreneur spirit, the next chapter will get you well on the road to becoming a successful self-publisher.

II
Developing a Marketing Plan

You may wonder why a chapter on developing a marketing plan appears early in this book. The reason is simple. You must *SELL* your book to be a successful self-publisher.

Every week, our Company receives telephone calls similar to the following:

> Yes, my name is Susie Doe. About a year ago, I published my own book titled "_____." Unfortunately, I have sold very few copies. I have a garage full of books and my husband is complaining about not having enough space. I am wondering whether your company would be interested in buying and selling my books?

Individuals often get all fired up about writing a book but give virtually no thought to selling it.

The key to successful self-publishing is to find a market where you can sell your book. You need to write a publication where there is sufficient demand to allow niche marketing. A niche market is necessary because most people do not have the financial resources needed to implement a broad based marketing program.

Advertising is essential and expensive. Find a market where you can take a direct aim using a rifle rather than a shotgun.

The best markets are covered by specialty magazines and catalogs. Examples of specialty markets are cooking, fishing, hunting, sewing, sailing, woodworking, etc.

Distribution is a key factor in your marketing plan. In the early years of your business, distribution decisions are easy. You simply must sell to anyone and everyone. As your business grows, distribution requires greater thought and planning.

The method that our Company has found so successful is to sell initially to the ultimate user. By advertising directly to organizations and readers, you will create demand at the lowest level. As your book grows in popularity, people will start going to bookstores and placing special orders. Bookstores will in turn order your book from their jobber or distributor. Persons will also be requesting your book at libraries who will order it from their suppliers. Over a period of several years, distributors and jobbers will be purchasing books from you for redistribution to their customers.

Our business began as 100% retail using direct mail and is now mainly wholesale. While sales to wholesalers offer lower profit margins, the volume generated by wholesalers provides overall greater profitability. Shipments in volume provide many efficiencies in paperwork, packaging and shipping. More importantly, wholesalers provide the volume you need to negotiate substantial quantity discounts with your printer. The lower margins to wholesalers are more than offset by higher book sales and lower manufacturing and distribution costs.

Although distribution through wholesalers offers the greatest opportunities for growth, there is one area of concern. You need to be careful about developing most of your sales through one or two large distributors. A business whose continued prosperity is dependent upon one or two large accounts is extremely vulnerable. If just one large account ceases to buy your book or goes bankrupt, your business could be in serious jeopardy.

A broad customer base is critical to your long-term success. Try to keep your business well-balanced among as many accounts as possible.

You will not want to overlook a number of markets. They are government, libraries, schools and seminars. By selling only one book to a high ranking person in a government agency or the military, you can create thousands of additional sales. Persons who see your book in a library will often purchase it. The use of your book in one college course can quickly spread to other campuses. A seminar leader who mentions your book can stimulate tremendous sales.

In short, your goal should be to create initial demand with direct buyers and eventually gain the support and distribution of many major wholesalers.

As your business prospers, you can expect to receive all kinds of inquiries. People will want to make appointments to somehow get involved in your business.

You will receive suggestions from persons who want to change *your* book. People may contact you and want to argue a certain subject in your book. We have had numerous requests for permission to copy one of our books or transfer our writings to computer disks.

As a general rule, we have found it advisable to politely and promptly decline most requests concerning reproductions, transfers or changes in our publications. If you give permission to reproduce several pages, you will invariably receive an additional request to reproduce the whole chapter. If you respond favorably to a suggested change, some people will virtually rewrite sections of your book which can lead to all types of problems.

You can spend a tremendous amount of time handling inquiries from outsiders. It's best to refuse outside assistance and devote your energies to improving your business.

You can also expect to receive requests from other writers to publish their books. We believe it is best to avoid publishing the works of other authors.

If you get involved with outside writers, you are likely to encounter many problems. The very nature of publishing provides unlimited potential for disputes.

All your efforts should be devoted to making your book or books a big success.

III
Choosing a Subject and Title

The choice of a subject is largely influenced by your knowledge and experience. The number one rule is to select a subject that you really know. Everyone is knowledgeable about something.

Keep in mind that your subject must fall into a category where it will sell. In order to sell, you must provide information that will fulfill a demand, satisfy a need or create interest. Nonfiction is considered to provide the best opportunity for success in self-publishing.

Our Company receives numerous inquiries every year from persons who are writing a book because of their strong interest in a subject. A book based on interest alone may provide tremendous satisfaction when discussing it with friends around a coffee table. However, selecting a subject solely on the basis of interest may lead to a commercial disaster. If you wish to make a profit, you must select a subject that has marketability. A keen interest in a subject which also has a big sales potential is a winning combination.

Unless you plan to publish annual editions, we suggest that you avoid subjects that relate to current laws, tax codes, government regulations and fast changing technology. Subjects that are based on ever changing circumstances can become obsolete before the book comes off the press.

For example, we recently reviewed a manuscript regarding financial planning for the elderly. It was our opinion that the contents were based largely on current federal and state tax regulations and interest rates which could change dramatically during the book's retail shelf life. Large publishing firms can publish works on timely subjects but it is a dangerous area for most self-publishers.

Do not be discouraged by the existence of other books on your subject. It is virtually impossible to write a nonfiction book on a subject that has not been previously published. No other author has your education, experience and abilities.

One of the safest subjects for beginners is "How To" books. In addition to direct sales, "How To" books provide excellent sales opportunities with outlets such as pet shops, building supply houses, garden centers, etc.

Libraries are also large purchasers of "How To" books. We recently used our computer to scan the catalog listings of major libraries. By using the search words "How To" we found an astonishing number of titles on a wide variety of subjects.

"How To" books offer great opportunities for specialization as illustrated by the following title possibilities:

> How To Teach Your Dog To Retrieve
> How To Teach Your Hunting Dog To Retrieve
> How To Teach Your Labrador To Retrieve
> How To Teach Your Labrador To Retrieve Ducks

Try to choose a title that will serve as an advertisement in itself. A title should generally be self-explanatory. A subtitle may be appropriate whenever it clarifies the main title or adds to sales appeal.

When selecting a title, we suggest that you engage the services of a title search firm. For a nominal fee, you can have a thorough search conducted to ensure that your chosen title does not already exist.

After you have selected your subject and title, you will want to closely follow all developments in the field. Read everything that relates to your subject. Clip and file all magazine and newspaper articles. It's better to file the complete article rather than sections.

In the business world, the emphasis is on "new." A new book on a reasonably researched subject is certain to attract attention simply because it offers a fresh look at perhaps an old subject.

IV
Writing the Manuscript

Before beginning your manuscript, imagine that you are standing in a bookstore eager to purchase a book on the subject which you are writing about. What would you as the buyer want to read? As a buyer, what would make your book stand out?

Features that could influence the buyer to select your book might include the following:

> clever and meaningful title
> unique or unusual subject
> attractive cover
> quality of printing
> easily readable with short sentences and
>   paragraphs
> pictures
> index
> testimonials
> reasonable price

After getting into the mind-set of a buyer, you are ready to begin your manuscript.

The first requirement is to write a Table of Contents by chapter. This outline will most likely change significantly as you get well into the book. However, the outline will give you a road map of where you are going. We suggest that you purchase a large three ring notebook and use dividers to mark your chapters.

Many writers prefer to write their book directly on a word processor. I have found it easier to write on large legal pads and then transfer the information to a word processor. It seems that writing on a pad lets you work anywhere in a more relaxed position.

When using the word processor, be sure to place a retrieval code at the top of each page. Nothing is more frustrating than to be unable to locate a previously typed page.

As you write your manuscript, you may often encounter writer's block. It will seem that no matter how hard you try, the creative processes just won't work. In these situations, we have found that it's best to leave your writing and go on to something else.

Sometimes you will write paragraphs that you believe are terrific. However, the same words may seem terrible the next day. Your writing needs to age by the hour, day and week in order to achieve your best effort.

Try to keep writing on your subject. Many authors run out of material and use irrelevant "fillers" to "pad" the book. Problems arise when a potential book buyer is flipping through your book. If the prospective buyer focuses in on unrelated or irrelevant information, he or she may quickly conclude that the book is not worth buying.

We believe it is best to write a short book in a concise manner than to produce a larger book padded with fillers. Sections such as glossaries and suggested readings should be kept to a reasonable level. As a general rule, we believe your manuscript should be a minimum of 100 printed pages.

We strongly recommend that you avoid areas where you are not qualified. For example, in Chapter VIII on organizing your business, we will not discuss the various types of business organizations and make a recommendation because we are not qualified. Instead, we suggest that you contact an attorney. Moreover, laws and tax regulations vary by state and it is difficult to be completely accurate on some subjects when discussed on a national basis.

In preparing your manuscript, keep in mind that your writings are subject to the laws of the land. It is essential that you read a current book on writing and the law. You should have a general understanding of the laws relating to defamation, "fair use" of other publications, plagiarism and copyright. While you cannot expect to become professionally qualified, you should possess enough knowledge to know whether you need to consult an attorney who specializes in copyright law.

When choosing words, it is often tempting to use large words. My rule of thumb is to use the dictionary for spelling, not meanings. If the author has to check the dictionary for the meaning of a word, it should not be used in the first place.

In short, you want to follow the style guidelines used by magazines and newspapers. We highly recommend the "U.S. News & World Report Stylebook For Writers and Editors" along with "The Associated Press Stylebook and Libel Manual."

Use short words with short paragraphs. Try to keep the book moving by using active verbs as much as possible. Every now and then, you need to stop and ask yourself "will this be of interest to the reader?"

We have found it useful to ask a trusted and respected friend to read your drafts. We suggest you ask a person who would represent the typical buyer. Many times another person will take an entirely different meaning from a paragraph or sentence which will obviously require revision.

With regard to spelling, you will want to use one of the computer software programs. However, spelling verification programs must be used with extreme caution. Words have many different meanings and uses.

Do not rely on printing firms for proofreading. Printers merely print whatever copy they receive.

It is always disappointing to discover post-printing spelling errors which we have experienced on more than one occasion. One of our earlier books had "Foreword" spelled "Forward." A good tip for your preliminary proofreading is verify each word by reading the book backwards.

After your manuscript has been prepared to the best of your ability, you are ready to select a typesetter. Although desktop publishing is very popular, we believe quite strongly that a professional typesetter who specializes in books is your best investment. Professionals keep abreast of current styles and they will make your book appear as good and hopefully better than similar publications in the marketplace. Appearance is vital because you need to impress reviewers in order to get free publicity.

Upon completion of the typesetting, you will be provided with proof pages. These pages will need to be thoroughly proofread.

Proofreading is a serious job and really belongs with the professionals. University English departments and printers will often recommend a good proofreader. The money spent with a skilled proofreader is a good investment.

Typesetters make mistakes in layout and style. Sometimes you can concentrate so much on spelling that you fail to correct errors in style, table of contents, page numbering, etc. You want to make sure that all your headings are in perfect alignment and in the same boldness and type.

A good index of your book is vital particularly if you are writing a reference book. Libraries prefer books with indexes.

You will need to wait until the text is in its final typeset before preparing an index. You can use a computer or file cards. Our preferred method of preparing an index is to begin with page one and write the subject and page number on a separate file card. After reviewing each page, you will have accumulated a pile of cards. The cards can be assembled in alphabetical order by subject. We suggest that you attempt to achieve a balance among your subjects. In general, we recommend a long rather than a short index.

V

Obtaining Licenses, Industry Registrations and Copyrights

As a publisher, it will be necessary for you to obtain a number of registrations. We suggest that you apply for the needed authorizations in the following order.

1. VENDOR'S LICENSE AND PERMITS

   Request a vendor's license or similar permit from your local and/or state governments.

2. UPC NUMBER

   Obtain a uniform product code number by joining the Uniform Product Code Council, Inc. The UPC will assign you an identification number and numbering system character which will be printed on the back of your cover. The number is used to record products as they move through the distribution system to the ultimate consumer.

3. ISBN NUMBER

   Obtain an International Standard Book Number (ISBN) from the R. R. Bowker Company. This number identifies the publisher, title and other pertinent information. Each title and edition requires a separate ISBN number. You will then need to contact one of a number of firms who will provide you with a bar code symbol incorporating the ISBN number for printing on the back cover with your UPC number.

When you are notified of your ISBN number, you will receive other forms from various industry sources requesting advance information on your forthcoming publication. It is very important that you promptly complete and return all forms requesting information on your book. The data is used to compile directories which are routinely used by booksellers and libraries.

4. SAN NUMBER

A Standard Account Number is a code assigned to various types of firms and organizations in the book industry such as publishers, book dealers, libraries, etc. Numbers are assigned by the R. R. Bowker Company.

5. LIBRARY OF CONGRESS CATALOG NUMBER

You must apply for a Library of Congress Catalog Number in the year preceding your year of publication. You need to receive this number prior to typesetting because it must be printed on the reverse side of the title page. A Library of Congress Catalog Number application is included in this chapter.

6. COPYRIGHT

Apply for a copyright registration. Your book must be published with the approved copyright notice properly printed on the reverse side of the title page. You can find the proper wording from the application appearing in this chapter.

We have not included the addresses for obtaining some of the above information because they are subject to change. In this respect, we suggest that you join The International Association of Independent Publishers (COSMEP). For nominal dues, you will receive a monthly newsletter which will keep you well informed of industry trends and developments. The association offers a backlist of newsletters containing specific subjects. As a member, you may also contact the association to learn of general industry information such as addresses for obtaining various identification numbers, etc. Libraries can also assist you in providing current addresses for obtaining general publishing information.

HOW WILL I KNOW IF MY APPLICATION WAS RECEIVED?

You will not receive an acknowledgement that your application has been received—the Office receives over 600,000 applications annually—but you can expect **within 16 weeks of submission** (normally much more quickly):

- A certificate of registration to indicate the work has been registered, or
- A letter or telephone call from a Copyright Office staff member if further information is needed; or, if the application cannot be accepted, a letter explaining why it has been rejected.

If you want to know when the Copyright Office receives your material, send it by registered or certified mail and request a return receipt from the Postal Service. Due to the large volume of mail received by the Office daily, **you should allow at least 3 weeks for the return of your receipt.**

WHAT IS THE STATUS OF MY APPLICATION?

We cannot provide free information about the status of applications that have been in the Copyright Office fewer than 16 weeks. If you must have this information sooner, contact the Certifications and Documents Section, which can provide this information upon payment of applicable fees.

WHEN IS MY REGISTRATION EFFECTIVE?

A copyright registration is effective on the date that all the required elements (application, fee, and deposit) in acceptable form are received in the Copyright Office, regardless of the length of time it takes the Copyright Office to process the application and mail the certificate of registration. You do not have to receive your certificate before you publish or produce your work, nor do you need permission from the Copyright Office to place a notice of copyright on your material.

HOW MANY FORMS MAY I RECEIVE?

Because of budget restrictions we can no longer send unlimited quantities of our application forms and publications. If you need additional application forms or circulars, you may order a limited supply by calling the Copyright Office Hotline anytime day or night at (202)707-9100 and leaving a message on the recorder. Please allow 2-3 weeks for delivery of your order.

We encourage you to photocopy our circulars and other informational material. You may also photocopy blank application forms. Many local public libraries have a master set of copyright application forms available to be photocopied. However, photocopied forms submitted to the Copyright Office must be clear, legible, and on a good grade of 8 1/2-inch by 11-inch white paper, suitable for automatic feeding through a photocopier. The forms should be printed, preferably in black ink, head to head (so that when you turn the sheet over, the top of page 2 is directly behind the top of page 1). **Forms not meeting these requirements will be returned.**

HOW DO I MAIL MATERIAL TO THE COPYRIGHT OFFICE?

Please use the following address when sending us mail:

Register of Copyrights
Copyright Office
Library of Congress
Washington, D.C. 20559-6000

Include your ZIP Code in your return address. Also, please supply your daytime telephone number. Make certain that you send your nonrefundable filing fee, your completed application form, and your nonreturnable deposit (copies, phonorecords, or identifying material) **in the same package.**

We suggest that you contact your local Post Office for information about mailing these materials at lower cost fourth-class postage rates.

COPYRIGHT PUBLIC INFORMATION OFFICE: (202) 707-3000; TTY (202) 707-6737

SL-9 March 1994 – 250,000

☆U.S. GOVERNMENT PRINTING OFFICE: 1994-301-241/80,059

⊘ Filling Out Application Form TX

Detach and read these instructions before completing this form. Make sure all applicable spaces have been filled in before you return this form.

BASIC INFORMATION

When to Use This Form: Use Form TX for registration of published or unpublished non-dramatic literary works, excluding periodicals or serial issues. This class includes a wide variety of works: fiction, non-fiction, poetry, textbooks, reference works, directories, catalogs, advertising copy, compilations of information, and computer programs. For periodicals and serials, use Form SE.

Deposit to Accompany Application: An application for copyright registration must be accompanied by a deposit consisting of copies or phonorecords representing the entire work for which registration is to be made. The following are the general deposit requirements as set forth in the statute:

Unpublished Work: Deposit one complete copy (or phonorecord).

Published Work: Deposit two complete copies or one phonorecord of the best edition.

Work First Published Outside the United States: Deposit one complete copy (or phonorecord) of the first foreign edition.

Contribution to a Collective Work: Deposit one complete copy (or phonorecord) of the best edition of the collective work.

The Copyright Notice: For works first published on or after March 1, 1989, the law provides that a copyright notice in a specified form "may be placed on all publicly distributed copies from which the work can be visually perceived." Use of the copyright notice is the responsibility of the copyright owner and does not require advance permission from the Copyright Office. The required form of the notice for copies generally consists of three elements: (1) the symbol "©", or the word "Copyright," or the abbreviation "Copr."; (2) the year of first publication; and (3) the name of the owner of copyright. For example: "© 1989 Jane Cole." The notice is to be affixed to the copies "in such manner and location as to give reasonable notice of the claim of copyright." Works first published prior to March 1, 1989, **must** carry the notice or risk loss of copyright protection.

For information about notice requirements for works published before March 1, 1989, or other copyright information, write: Information Section LM-401, Copyright Office, Library of Congress, Washington, D.C. 20559.

LINE-BY-LINE INSTRUCTIONS

1 SPACE 1: Title

Title of This Work: Every work submitted for copyright registration must be given a title to identify that particular work. If the copies or phonorecords of the work bear a title (or an identifying phrase that could serve as a title), transcribe that wording *completely* and *exactly* on the application. Indexing of the registration and future identification of the work will depend on the information you give here.

Previous or Alternative Titles: Complete this space if there are any additional titles for the work under which someone searching for the registration might be likely to look, or under which a document pertaining to the work might be recorded.

Publication as a Contribution: If the work being registered is a contribution to a periodical, serial, or collection, give the title of the contribution in the "Title of this Work" space. Then, in the line headed "Publication as a Contribution," give information about the collective work in which the contribution appeared.

2 SPACE 2: Author(s)

General Instructions: After reading these instructions, decide who are the "authors" of this work for copyright purposes. Then, unless the work is a "collective work," give the requested information about every "author" who contributed any appreciable amount of copyrightable matter to this version of the work. If you need further space, request Continuation sheets. In the case of a collective work, such as an anthology, collection of essays, or encyclopedia, give information about the author of the collective work as a whole.

Name of Author: The fullest form of the author's name should be given. Unless the work was "made for hire," the individual who actually created the work is its "author." In the case of a work made for hire, the statute provides that "the employer or other person for whom the work was prepared is considered the author."

What is a "Work Made for Hire"? A "work made for hire" is defined as: (1) "a work prepared by an employee within the scope of his or her employment"; or (2) "a work specially ordered or commissioned for use as a contribution to a collective work, as a part of a motion picture or other audiovisual work, as translation, as a supplementary work, as a compilation, as an instructional text, as a test, as answer material for a test, or as an atlas, if the parties expressly agree in a written instrument signed by them that the work shall be considered a work made for hire." If you have checked "Yes" to indicate that the work was "made for hire," you must give the full legal name of the employer (or other person for whom the work was prepared). You may also include the name of the employee along with the name of the employer (for example: "Elste Publishing Co., employer for hire of John Ferguson").

"Anonymous" or "Pseudonymous" Work: An author's contribution to a work is "anonymous" if that author is not identified on the copies or phonorecords of the work. An author's contribution to a work is "pseudonymous" if that author is identified on the copies or phonorecords under a fictitious name. If the work is "anonymous" you may: (1) leave the line blank; or (2) state "anonymous" on the line; or (3) reveal the author's identity. If the work is "pseudonymous" you may: (1) leave the line blank; or (2) give the pseudonym and identify it as such (for example: "Huntley Haverstock, pseudonym"); or (3) reveal the author's name, making clear which is the real name and which is the pseudonym (for example: "Judith Barton, whose pseudonym is Madeline Elster"). However, the citizenship or domicile of the author **must** be given in all cases.

Dates of Birth and Death: If the author is dead, the statute requires that the year of death be included in the application unless the work is anonymous or pseudonymous. The author's birth date is optional, but is useful as a form of identification. Leave this space blank if the author's contribution was a "work made for hire."

Author's Nationality or Domicile: Give the country of which the author is a citizen, or the country in which the author is domiciled. Nationality or domicile **must** be given in all cases.

Nature of Authorship: After the words "Nature of Authorship" give a brief general statement of the nature of this particular author's contribution to the work. Examples: "Entire text", "Coauthor of entire text", "Chapters 11-14", Editorial revisions", "Compilation and English translation", "New text."

SPACE 3: Creation and Publication

General Instructions: Do not confuse "creation" with "publication." Every application for copyright registration must state "the year in which creation of the work was completed." Give the date and nation of first publication only if the work has been published.

Creation: Under the statute, a work is "created" when it is fixed in a copy or phonorecord for the first time. Where a work has been prepared over a period of time, the part of the work existing in fixed form on a particular date constitutes the created work on that date. The date you give here should be the year in which the author completed the particular version for which registration is now being sought, even if other versions exist or if further changes or additions are planned.

Publication: The statute defines "publication" as "the distribution of copies or phonorecords of a work to the public by sale or other transfer of ownership, by rental, lease, or lending"; a work is also "published" if there has been an offering to distribute copies or phonorecords to a group of persons for purposes of further distribution, public performance, or public display." Give the full date (month, day, year) when, and the country where, publication first occurred. If first publication took place simultaneously in the United States and other countries, it is sufficient to state "U.S.A."

SPACE 4: Claimant(s)

Name(s) and Address(es) of Copyright Claimant(s): Give the name(s) and address(es) of the copyright claimant(s) in this work even if the claimant is the same as the author. Copyright in a work belongs initially to the author of the work (including, in the case of a work made for hire, the employer or other person for whom the work was prepared). The copyright claimant is either the author of the work or a person or organization to whom the copyright initially belonging to the author has been transferred.

Transfer: The statute provides that, if the copyright claimant is not the author, the application for registration must contain "a brief statement of how the claimant obtained ownership of the copyright." If any copyright claimant named in space 4 is not an author named in space 2, give a brief statement explaining how the claimant(s) obtained ownership of the copyright. Examples: "By written contract"; "Transfer of all rights by author"; "Assignment"; "By will." Do not attach transfer documents or other attachments or riders.

SPACE 5: Previous Registration

General Instructions: The questions in space 5 are intended to find out whether an earlier registration has been made for this work and, if so, whether there is any basis for a new registration. As a general rule, only one basic copyright registration can be made for the same version of a particular work.

Same Version: If this version is substantially the same as the work covered by a previous registration, a second registration is not generally possible unless: (1) the work has been registered in unpublished form and a second registration is now being sought to cover this first published edition; or (2) someone other than the author is identified as copyright claimant in the earlier registration, and the author is now seeking registration in his or her own name. If either of these two exceptions apply, check the appropriate box and give the earlier registration number and date. Otherwise, do not submit Form TX; instead, write the Copyright Office for information about supplementary registration or recordation of transfers of copyright ownership.

Changed Version: If the work has been changed, and you are now seeking registration to cover the additions or revisions, check the last box in space 5, give the earlier registration number and date, and complete both parts of space 6 in accordance with the instructions below.

Previous Registration Number and Date: If more than one previous registration has been made for the work, give the number and date of the latest registration.

6 SPACE 6: Derivative Work or Compilation

General Instructions: Complete space 6 if this work is a "changed version," "compilation," or "derivative work," and if it incorporates one or more earlier works that have already been published or registered for copyright, or that have fallen into the public domain. A "compilation" is defined as "a work formed by the collection and assembling of preexisting materials or of data that are selected, coordinated, or arranged in such a way that the resulting work as a whole constitutes an original work of authorship." A "derivative work" is "a work based on one or more preexisting works." Examples of derivative works include translations, fictionalizations, abridgments, condensations, or "any other form in which a work may be recast, transformed, or adapted." Derivative works also include works "consisting of editorial revisions, annotations, or other modifications" if these changes, as a whole, represent an original work of authorship.

Preexisting Material (space 6a): For derivative works, complete this space and space 6b. In space 6a identify the preexisting work that has been recast, transformed, or adapted. An example of preexisting material might be: "Russian version of Goncharov's 'Oblomov'." Do not complete space 6a for compilations.

Material Added to This Work (space 6b): Give a brief, general statement of the new material covered by the copyright claim for which registration is sought. Derivative work examples include: "Foreword, editing, critical annotations"; "Translation"; "Chapters 11-17." If the work is a **compilation**, describe both the compilation itself and the material that has been compiled. Example: "Compilation of certain 1917 Speeches by Woodrow Wilson." A work may be both a derivative work and compilation, in which case a sample statement might be: "Compilation and additional new material."

7 SPACE 7: Manufacturing Provisions

Due to the expiration of the Manufacturing Clause of the copyright law on June 30, 1986, this space has been deleted.

8 SPACE 8: Reproduction for Use of Blind or Physically Handicapped Individuals

General Instructions: One of the major programs of the Library of Congress is to provide Braille editions and special recordings of works for the exclusive use of the blind and physically handicapped. In an effort to simplify and speed up the copyright licensing procedures that are a necessary part of this program, section 710 of the copyright statute provides for the establishment of a voluntary licensing system to be tied in with copyright registration. Copyright Office regulations provide that you may grant a license for such reproduction and distribution solely for the use of persons who are certified by competent authority as unable to read normal printed material as a result of physical limitations. The license is entirely voluntary, nonexclusive, and may be terminated upon 90 days notice.

How to Grant the License: If you wish to grant it, check one of the three boxes in space 8. Your check in one of these boxes, together with your signature in space 10, will mean that the Library of Congress can proceed to reproduce and distribute under the license without further paperwork. For further information, write for Circular R63.

9,10,11 SPACE 9, 10, 11: Fee, Correspondence, Certification, Return Address

Fee: Copyright fees are adjusted at 5-year intervals, based on increases or decreases in the Consumer Price Index. The next adjustment is due in 1995. Contact the Copyright Office in January 1995 for the new fee schedule.
Deposit Account: If you maintain a Deposit Account in the Copyright Office, identify it in space 9. Otherwise leave the space blank and send the fee of $20 with your application and deposit.

Correspondence (space 9): This space should contain the name, address, area code, and telephone number of the person to be consulted if correspondence about this application becomes necessary.

Certification (space 10): The application can not be accepted unless it bears the date and the **handwritten signature** of the author or other copyright claimant, or of the owner of exclusive right(s), or of the duly authorized agent of author, claimant, or owner of exclusive right(s).

Address for Return of Certificate (space 11): The address box must be completed legibly since the certificate will be returned in a window envelope.

FORM TX

For a Literary Work
UNITED STATES COPYRIGHT OFFICE

REGISTRATION NUMBER

TX	TXU

EFFECTIVE DATE OF REGISTRATION

_____ _____ _____
Month   Day   Year

DO NOT WRITE ABOVE THIS LINE. IF YOU NEED MORE SPACE, USE A SEPARATE CONTINUATION SHEET.

1

TITLE OF THIS WORK ▼

PREVIOUS OR ALTERNATIVE TITLES ▼

PUBLICATION AS A CONTRIBUTION If this work was published as a contribution to a periodical, serial, or collection, give information about the collective work in which the contribution appeared.   **Title of Collective Work ▼**

If published in a periodical or serial give: **Volume ▼**   **Number ▼**   **Issue Date ▼**   **On Pages ▼**

2

a

NAME OF AUTHOR ▼

DATES OF BIRTH AND DEATH
Year Born ▼   Year Died ▼

Was this contribution to the work a "work made for hire"?
☐ Yes
☐ No

AUTHOR'S NATIONALITY OR DOMICILE
Name of Country
OR { Citizen of ▶ _____
     Domiciled in▶ _____

WAS THIS AUTHOR'S CONTRIBUTION TO THE WORK
Anonymous?   ☐ Yes ☐ No
Pseudonymous? ☐ Yes ☐ No

If the answer to either of these questions is "Yes," see detailed instructions.

NATURE OF AUTHORSHIP Briefly describe nature of material created by this author in which copyright is claimed. ▼

NOTE

Under the law, the "author" of a "work made for hire" is generally the employer, not the employee (see instructions). For any part of this work that was "made for hire" check "Yes" in the space provided, give the employer (or other person for whom the work was prepared) as "Author" of that part, and leave the space for dates of birth and death blank.

b

NAME OF AUTHOR ▼

DATES OF BIRTH AND DEATH
Year Born ▼   Year Died ▼

Was this contribution to the work a "work made for hire"?
☐ Yes
☐ No

AUTHOR'S NATIONALITY OR DOMICILE
Name of Country
OR { Citizen of ▶ _____
     Domiciled in▶ _____

WAS THIS AUTHOR'S CONTRIBUTION TO THE WORK
Anonymous?   ☐ Yes ☐ No
Pseudonymous? ☐ Yes ☐ No

If the answer to either of these questions is "Yes," see detailed instructions.

NATURE OF AUTHORSHIP Briefly describe nature of material created by this author in which copyright is claimed. ▼

c

NAME OF AUTHOR ▼

DATES OF BIRTH AND DEATH
Year Born ▼   Year Died ▼

Was this contribution to the work a "work made for hire"?
☐ Yes
☐ No

AUTHOR'S NATIONALITY OR DOMICILE
Name of Country
OR { Citizen of ▶ _____
     Domiciled in▶ _____

WAS THIS AUTHOR'S CONTRIBUTION TO THE WORK
Anonymous?   ☐ Yes ☐ No
Pseudonymous? ☐ Yes ☐ No

If the answer to either of these questions is "Yes," see detailed instructions.

NATURE OF AUTHORSHIP Briefly describe nature of material created by this author in which copyright is claimed. ▼

3

a

YEAR IN WHICH CREATION OF THIS WORK WAS COMPLETED This information must be given in all cases.
◀ Year

b **DATE AND NATION OF FIRST PUBLICATION OF THIS PARTICULAR WORK**
Complete this information ONLY if this work has been published.
Month ▶ _____ Day ▶ _____ Year ▶ _____
_____ ◀ Nat

4

See instructions before completing this space.

COPYRIGHT CLAIMANT(S) Name and address must be given even if the claimant is the same as the author given in space 2. ▼

TRANSFER If the claimant(s) named here in space 4 is (are) different from the author(s) named in space 2, give a brief statement of how the claimant(s) obtained ownership of the copyright. ▼

DO NOT WRITE HERE OFFICE USE ONLY

APPLICATION RECEIVED

ONE DEPOSIT RECEIVED

TWO DEPOSITS RECEIVED

FUNDS RECEIVED

MORE ON BACK ▶ • Complete all applicable spaces (numbers 5-11) on the reverse side of this page.
• See detailed instructions.   • Sign the form at line 10.

DO NOT WRITE HE
Page 1 of _____ pag

CORRESPONDENCE
Yes

FOR
COPYRIGHT
OFFICE
USE
ONLY

DO NOT WRITE ABOVE THIS LINE. IF YOU NEED MORE SPACE, USE A SEPARATE CONTINUATION SHEET.

PREVIOUS REGISTRATION Has registration for this work, or for an earlier version of this work, already been made in the Copyright Office?

☐ **Yes** ☐ No If your answer is "Yes," why is another registration being sought? (Check appropriate box) ▼

a. ☐ This is the first published edition of a work previously registered in unpublished form.

b. ☐ This is the first application submitted by this author as copyright claimant.

c. ☐ This is a changed version of the work, as shown by space 6 on this application.

If your answer is "Yes," give: **Previous Registration Number** ▼   **Year of Registration** ▼

5

DERIVATIVE WORK OR COMPILATION Complete both space 6a and 6b for a derivative work; complete only 6b for a compilation.

a. **Preexisting Material** Identify any preexisting work or works that this work is based on or incorporates. ▼

b. **Material Added to This Work** Give a brief, general statement of the material that has been added to this work and in which copyright is claimed. ▼

See instructions
before completing
this space.

6

—space deleted—

7

REPRODUCTION FOR USE OF BLIND OR PHYSICALLY HANDICAPPED INDIVIDUALS A signature on this form at space 10 and a check in one of the boxes here in space 8 constitutes a non-exclusive grant of permission to the Library of Congress to reproduce and distribute solely for the blind and physically handicapped and under the conditions and limitations prescribed by the regulations of the Copyright Office: (1) copies of the work identified in space 1 of this application in Braille (or similar tactile symbols); or (2) phonorecords embodying a fixation of a reading of that work; or (3) both.

a ☐ Copies and Phonorecords   b ☐ Copies Only   c ☐ Phonorecords Only   See instructions.

8

DEPOSIT ACCOUNT If the registration fee is to be charged to a Deposit Account established in the Copyright Office, give name and number of Account.

Name ▼   **Account Number** ▼

9

CORRESPONDENCE Give name and address to which correspondence about this application should be sent.   Name/Address/Apt/City/State/ZIP ▼

Be sure to
give your
daytime phone
◄ number

Area Code and Telephone Number ▶

CERTIFICATION* I, the undersigned, hereby certify that I am the

Check only one ▶

☐ author
☐ other copyright claimant
☐ owner of exclusive right(s)
☐ authorized agent of _____

of the work identified in this application and that the statements made by me in this application are correct to the best of my knowledge.

Name of author or other copyright claimant, or owner of exclusive right(s) ▲

Typed or printed name and date ▼ If this application gives a date of publication in space 3, do not sign and submit it before that date.

date ▶

Handwritten signature (X) ▼

10

MAIL CERTIFICATE TO

Name ▼

Number/Street/Apartment Number ▼

City/State/ZIP ▼

Certificate
will be
mailed in
window
envelope

YOU MUST:
• Complete all necessary spaces
• Sign your application in space 10

SEND ALL 3 ELEMENTS IN THE SAME PACKAGE:
1. Application form
2. Nonrefundable $20 filing fee in check or money order payable to *Register of Copyrights*
3. Deposit material

MAIL TO:
Register of Copyrights
Library of Congress
Washington, D.C. 20559-6000

The Copyright Office has the authority to adjust fees at 5-year intervals, based on changes in the Consumer Price Index. The next adjustment is due in 1996. Please contact the Copyright Office after July 1995 to determine the actual fee schedule.

11

17 U.S.C. § 506(e): Any person who knowingly makes a false representation of a material fact in the application for copyright registration provided for by section 409, or in any written statement filed in connection with the application, shall be fined not more than $2,500.

July 1993—400,000   ✿ PRINTED ON RECYCLED PAPER   ☆U.S. GOVERNMENT PRINTING OFFICE: 1993-342-582/80,020

REQUEST FOR PREASSIGNMENT OF LIBRARY OF CONGRESS CATALOG CARD NUMBER

NOTE: *Card numbers cannot be preassigned to books which are already published. Works that receive a preassigned Library of Congress catalog card number are not eligible to receive cataloging in publication data for that same edition of the work.*

DATE: _____

PUBLISHER'S NAME ON TITLE PAGE: _____

YOUR NAME: _____ PHONE NUMBER: _____

Type or print clearly the complete address to which the preassigned card number should be sent. (This will be your return mailing label.)

┌   ┐

└   ┘

FOR CIP OFFICE USE

Library of Congress Catalog
Card Number preassigned is:

Transcribe the information in items 1-8 exactly in the form and order in which it will appear on the title or copyright pages of the printed book. Use only those abbreviations which will actually appear on these pages. **(Please attach a copy of the proposed title page, if available.)**

1. Author(s) _____

2. Editor(s) _____

3. Title _____

4. Subtitle _____

5. Edition (exactly as printed in the publication, e.g. second edition, revised edition, etc.) _____

6. U.S. place of publication: City _____ State _____

7. Any copublisher(s) and place _____

8. Series title and numbering, exactly as printed in the publication _____

9. Approximate number of pages _____ 10. Number of volumes _____

11. ISBN (Hard cover) _____ ISBN (Paperback) _____

12. Proposed date of publication: Month _____ Year _____ 13. Language of text, if other than English _____

14. Does (or will) the title in item 3 appear at periodic intervals, e.g. annually, quarterly, etc.? ☐ Yes ☐ No

For each title which is preassigned a Library of Congress catalog card number, the Library of Congress requires one non-returnable complimentary copy of the best edition of the published book. If selected for the Library's collections, the book will be cataloged. A postage-free, self-addressed label will be sent with the preassigned card number for your convenience in mailing the required advance copy of the work as soon as printed. This copy is in addition to copyright deposit copies.

Send this form to: Library of Congress
Cataloging in Publication Division
101 Independence Ave., S.E.
Washington, DC 20540-4320

FOR CIP OFFICE USE ONLY.

Searching notes:

RECD: _____
ASGN: _____
SENT: _____
APIF: _____

607-7 (rev 3/93)

VI
Designing the Book

For economic reasons, you will probably want to publish a standard size softcover book. A book with good quality paper and an attractive cover is critical.

We recommend a softcover book because a hardcover book is simply too costly for a new publishing venture. Libraries are increasingly buying softcover books which they protect with heavy plastic covers.

You should be cautioned that a book cover using several colors along with professional artwork is very expensive. Colorful artwork and photography are costly to prepare and expensive to print.

The best covers incorporate large type on a simple cover. If you use small type, your book will not present a good image whenever it is reduced to a small photograph for promotional literature and catalogs. The title, subtitle and author's name should appear on the cover. The current style is to include only the author's name with no "by."

While we have sold hundreds of thousands of books with an imprinted plastic spine, this physical characteristic is suitable only for manuals that must lie flat. Bookstores simply do not want spiral-bound books.

The choice of paper is one of the biggest decisions which will affect the cost of your book. Printers offer paper in many weights, colors and qualities with prices that vary considerably. Printers will provide many sample papers for your selection.

The weight and bulk of paper will affect the thickness of your book. We recommend that you select two sample papers and request the printer to make dummy copies of your book using the same number of pages. You can make better decisions based on actual sample books.

Sometimes you can find tremendous bargains on paper. On several occasions, we have been able to purchase high quality paper at a very low cost because a large printer had excess paper remaining after a big printing run. Large printers also offer a house paper which they buy in huge quantities and make available at a very attractive price.

We suggest a book with perfect binding which means that the spine is flat. A flat spine is achieved by glueing the ends of sheets together. The spine should include the author's name, title and ISBN number.

With regard to testimonials, we believe they should only be used when the person is a recognized authority. Using a testimonial from a person who lacks recognition and authority may actually weaken your book's sales appeal. Whenever available, strong testimonials should be printed with permission on the covers.

It will be necessary to decide whether you wish to include information "about the author" along with a small photograph. Unless you are a recognized authority or have sound practical experience, we suggest you avoid including information on yourself. On the otherhand, if you are a vice president or higher of one of the nation's five hundred largest corporations, or have practical experience such as owning a chain of landscape outlets or have developed a large professional following, you will want to include information on yourself. It should appear on the lower back cover.

If you are fortunate to receive prepublication reviews, from a recognized magazine or newspaper, they should be printed with permission on the outside covers. Of course, a very powerful review should be printed on the front cover.

When printing reviews, it is not necessary to quote every word. Reviews can be extremely powerful by quoting just several words. You need to only list the name of the magazine or newspaper as the source and not the name of the reviewer.

The back cover should include your Uniform Product Code symbol along with your ISBN Number in the lower right corner.

In short, you want your book to be attractive and comply with the current style. Your goal is to make your book appear as good or better than the books offered by major publishers.

VII
Selecting a Printer

Book printing is a specialized business. In the early years of our venture, we made the mistake of going to a general commercial printer. Although commercial printers can produce a high quality product, they simply cannot compete from a cost standpoint with specialized book printers.

Book printers have the equipment and the know-how needed to manufacture a quality book at a low cost. We have found that book printers can offer prices 60 to 70% lower than reputable commercial printers. A major cost savings is due to the large quantity of paper which book printers purchase by the boxcar load. Using stock paper offered by large book printers provides tremendous cost savings.

By forwarding your manuscript to a number of book printers, you will receive quotes with wide variances. It is important to make sure that all printers are quoting on the same cover, paper weight and quantity. We believe a minimum order of 2,500 books is necessary in order to warrant serious price quotations by printers.

Do not limit potential printers to your geographic area. The prices quoted by some printers located hundreds of miles away may be substantially lower even after transportation costs are added. We have had excellent success with large printers located in the Southern United States.

Before issuing a purchase order, be sure to clarify the percent of over or underruns that will be accepted. You can generally plan on receiving a quantity that will be plus or minus ten percent.

You should also make certain that the selected printer will issue a credit for defective books. Our firm has used many printers ranging in size from the very smallest to the very largest. You can expect to receive copies which will have one or more of the following defects:

1. defective front or back covers
2. dog-eared pages
3. bent or creased pages
4. missing pages
5. printing is excessively light or dark
6. blurry printing

With a new printer, we suggest that you return the actual defective books. After you develop a relationship with a printer, they will normally require that you merely return title pages for full credit.

After your book is printed, you need to decide where the printing plates and camera ready copy are to be stored. If you are doing business with a well established printer, you may wish to have the printer store your materials. On the otherhand, you may find it desirable to keep the plates and camera ready copy in your complete custody. We prefer to store all plates and copy with the printer.

As additional printings or editions become necessary, it is always advisable to obtain new quotations. We have found that printers will often quote a low price to get your business and significantly raise prices on later printings.

In working with printers, we have learned from many years of experience that you need to continuously follow-up. Never assume that your printer has ordered the paper, covers, etc. We suggest that you periodically call your printer and make sure that all the components of your book, including press time, are on schedule. It's better to learn early of any problems and avoid any surprises.

With regard to flyer sheets, order forms and other basic printing needs, you will want to purchase these items from local printers. We believe it is advisable to do business with two local printers. By having two printing sources, you will be in a good position to compare prices, quality, etc. We have found that some printers will merely print the material provided whereas others will offer creative recommendations at no extra cost. Reliability and prompt delivery also vary widely among printers.

Selecting high quality printers at the best possible cost is essential to your publishing success.

VIII
Organizing and Locating the Business

The easiest approach to starting a business is to operate as a sole proprietor. In some states, establishing a sole proprietorship only requires that you obtain a vendor's license. The type of business organization will depend on your individual situation. You will want to seek the advice of an attorney and a tax specialist.

The forming of a corporation provides protection from business liability. An attorney will conduct a search to determine if there are any other companies with your chosen name.

You may wish to use the word "publications" in your company name rather than "publishing" or "press." We believe that "publications" is better because it will not be misleading in the advent that you add books from other publishers. The word "publishing" implies that you only publish.

Try to select a company name that conveys strength and reliability. Although many experts recommend that you do not include your name in the company's name, we believe this advice is debatable. Many persons enjoy dealing with the owner of a company.

It is important for your business to convey the image that it is a large and reputable firm. You do not want your customers to know that your "headquarters" may be your kitchen table. If you incorporate, you will be perceived as a larger publisher.

Once you obtain the required vendor's license or other certifications from local and state agencies, you will soon learn about taxes and small business. You will receive tax forms that you never knew existed. You will also learn that many of your major business decisions will be heavily influenced by tax considerations.

Our firm has used one of the nation's largest accounting firms since our first days of business. Using a well-known accounting firm is very expensive. However, we continue to believe that paying for the best tax advice is a sound business practice. Moreover, the resources of a national firm are becoming increasingly beneficial due to the growing number of state and international tax regulations. Hiring a recognized accounting firm is the one area where we believe that going first class is a smart investment.

Our business started in a basement but we soon encountered zoning problems. After a semitrailer delivered books to our home, a neighbor complained to the local zoning board and we were forced to rent a commercial location. After it became apparent that we had a flourishing business, we purchased a large commercial lot with a suitable building offering great opportunities for expansion. Incidentally, we are always amazed at the number of magazine articles on starting a home business which do not even mention possible zoning violations.

Persons who start a home based business need to review their insurance policies. Most homeowner's policies do not include coverage for business related equipment and inventories.

If you rent an office, you should consider a number of factors. You will not need an office in a high traffic area. However, you will want to be on the ground floor because books are heavy. It is also important to remember that books must be stored in a dry location which is not subject to wide changes in temperature. Books tend to absorb moisture and it is vital that they be properly stored.

The best approach is to start your business in the home and plan to eventually rent or purchase a building. A separate business location offers the following advantages:

1. fully tax deductible
2. no zoning concerns
3. more appropriate for hiring employees
4. simplified insurance coverage
5. easier to receive shipments by large trucks
6. easier to ship books by various carriers
7. provides a more productive work environment

Beginning with your early start-up days, it is important that you have someone who can operate the business in your absence. If an illness or other emergency should strike, you need to have competent backup. With more and more business being conducted by telephone and fax, you simply cannot close down your firm. Moreover, you need to take vacations from time to time without worrying about your business. Money spent for a competent and trusted backup person is a good investment.

Regardless of where you locate your office, we recommend that you rent a post office box. Try to get a number that may be easily remembered.

A post office box provides your company with a permanent address. If you relocate your business, your mailing address will not change.

Our Company continues to receive orders on forms that were printed a decade ago. Without a P.O. box, old order forms would be undeliverable.

We do not recommend that you rent a mail box at a private business. The danger of a private mail box allowing for a suite number is that the firm may go out of business leaving you with worthless stationery, flyer sheets and industry listings. When using a P.O. box in advertising and printed material, we suggest that you also include a street address because some buyers may be reluctant to order from a P.O. box number only.

With regard to financing, you need to have sufficient capital to successfully launch your business. It is absolutely true that you have to spend money to make money.

You must be in a position where you can fully concentrate on writing, printing and promoting your book. An attractive and well written book will not sell by itself. You must have the financial resources to undertake a strong publicity and marketing program that will yield many dividends.

In summary, you need sound legal, commercial and tax advice before starting your business.

IX
Equipping the Office

To operate efficiently, you will need a well equipped office and shipping area. Fortunately, the cost of most electronic office equipment has dropped dramatically in the past ten years.

Your first purchase should be a powerful personal computer. As your business grows, you will need to have greater computer capacity.

With respect to computers, we have learned from experience that it's best to consult with someone that you personally know or can absolutely trust. We have found that many computer firms will incorrectly advise that you need extensive computer equipment. In one situation, we were informed that our desired functions could only be accomplished by purchasing a costly new computer with greater capacity. However, a personal friend and computer expert was able to locate and adapt existing software which met our objective using the existing computer. Friendship saved us many thousands of dollars!

Be sure to select a high-speed printer. In this respect, make certain that the printer can print legibly through one original invoice and four copies. Sales personnel often will not even inquire about the number of copies you plan to print.

Many printers will quickly print through an original and four copies but will not print an attractive letter. The best situation is to have a high-speed printer for your forms along with a separate high quality laser printer for correspondence.

A facsimile machine is vital in modern day business. More and more of our orders are being received by fax. Never forget that when your day ends, businesses on the other side of the world are just beginning their day.

We recommend a high quality facsimile machine because it will be used extensively. We recently received a government order that measured 15 feet long in fax paper. The long document included 14 pages of government regulations, rules, conditions, etc.

Although a dedicated fax line is desirable, keep in mind that having a second telephone line for your fax machine will add to your overhead. As a starter, you might wish to consider a machine that can function using a single telephone line. With a single line, you merely press a button or activate an automatic control that will convert your line to the fax machine as needed. Upon completion of the fax transmission, the line will revert to the regular telephone line.

A quality typewriter is also essential. Although your computer can print letters and envelopes, there are many occasions where you will use the typewriter rather than pump up your computer.

A good tabletop copy machine is also critical. We have found that a name brand tabletop copier in the middle price range will provide excellent service for many years. A black and white copy machine will normally be suitable for your needs.

For big copying jobs, we recommend that you use the large machines available at specialized copy shops. Repairs on copy machines are costly and you want to keep wear to a minimum.

As your business grows, you may wish to consider purchasing a low-priced folding machine. Printers will charge extra for folding your flyer sheets. Over a relatively short period of time, a folding machine will prove to be a good investment.

SHIPPING EQUIPMENT AND SUPPLIES

In the shipping area, we suggest a long table with a water fed tape dispensing machine. For years we have used a machine that accepts 3-1/2" glass reinforced tape. Although reinforced tape is more costly, it is very strong and will ensure safe packaging. We also suggest that you purchase a paper cutter and a paper dispenser for rolls 18" wide. We also recommend a rack which you can make to hold large rolls of 3/16" bubbled plastic and 1/2" bubbled plastic.

You are also going to need a shipping scale. The best scales automatically compute the shipping cost by carrier. Electronic computer scales are very expensive and you may need to spend several hundred dollars for new computer prompts whenever a carrier changes its rates.

As a starter, we suggest a good quality electronic scale that will allow you to use the rate charts provided by carriers. Eventually, you will want to purchase a highly sophisticated computer scale which will automatically print numbered labels, shipping receipts and a manifest.

With regard to postage, do not use stamps because they convey the image of a kitchen table operation. Instead, you should use metered mail.

You can rent postage meters from various companies. However, a postage meter will increase your overhead. During the initial stages of your business, we suggest that you stamp "SPECIAL FOURTH CLASS" in red ink on your cartons and take them to the post office where metered stamps will be affixed.

The money spent on good office equipment is a sound investment. The better your equipment, the less chance for breakdowns and errors. Quality equipment will eliminate many problems and also reduce labor and repair costs.

TELEPHONE ANSWERING SERVICE

If you are operating your business as a sideline venture, you might wish to consider a telephone answering service. They will answer your phone in the name of your business and notify you of all calls. We once engaged a service that became very familiar with our business and would actually take orders.

In cases where your business is located in the Eastern time zone, it is important to recognize that the West Coast will continue to conduct normal business several hours after you close. Also, foreign callers often disregard time zones. In many situations, a telephone answering service can be very helpful. It is more professional to have a person answering your phone rather than an answering machine. Answering services are costly and it is advisable to compare prices.

PURCHASING SUPPLIES

In our early years of business, we purchased supplies from various catalog houses. Mail order catalogs offer a wide selection, good prices on small items and fast delivery.

Although we continue to buy some items from catalogs, most of our materials are purchased directly from local distributors. We have found that local wholesalers offer prices on bulky and heavy items which are much lower than catalog marketers. Catalogs often feature low prices but the total cost of shipping and handling on heavy and bulky products can far exceed the prices from local distributors.

STATIONERY AND BUSINESS CARDS

We recommend that you purchase high quality business stationery with an attractive letterhead and envelopes. You will also need a supply of business cards. Develop a color scheme and printing style which can be uniformly used for all your printing requirements.

X
Developing Publicity

A well planned publicity program is essential to your publishing success. The key element of your program is a well written publicity release.

We recommend that you begin your release by stating some kind of a problem. Your opening paragraph should concentrate on the reason for the book rather than the book itself. You then proceed to explain why your book will solve the problem.

Make your copy appear that it was already written by a newspaper editor. The best copy is concise and factual. Many editors especially at small publications will carry your exact wording. Your success will be higher if your copy can be lifted "as is."

Be sure to include a paragraph stating the price of the book and where it may be purchased. For example, "available at many bookstores (if true) or from *Name and address of your company.*"

It is vital that you clearly state the applicable postage and handling charges on direct sales from your company. We have experienced many situations where the editor includes the price of the book but fails to mention postage and handling charges.

We have reviewed all kinds of recommendations on how to layout a publicity release. We suggest that you print a publicity release on a single 8-1/2" by 11" high quality paper using a layout similar to the sample shown on the next page.

PUBLICITY RELEASE

(Date) _____

For Additional Information
Contact:
   Your Name
   Company Name
   Street Address
   P.O. Box Number
   City, State, Zip
   Phone Number
   Fax Number

SAMPLE PUBLICITY RELEASE

Traditional advice is to begin your publicity program well before the actual book is printed. Some publications particularly in the library market require galley proofs for review several months prior to publication. While prepublication publicity efforts are great for large firms, we have found that our approach produces excellent results.

Our time proven method to obtaining publicity is to wait until the first book comes off the press. The book should carry the same year copyright and be sent to the media early in January.

We recommend sending hundreds of complimentary copies along with a publicity release to the nation's magazines, newspapers and newsletters. You can obtain publication names and current addresses at a large library. The same information may also be purchased from several directory companies.

To add a touch of class, we suggest that you enclose a card with each complimentary book. We suggest a card printed on high quality paper which is heavy and ivory in color. The card should be folded over the top of the front cover. We have experienced excellent success with the card shown on the next page.

If your financial situation will not allow the mailing of complimentary copies, you can use an alternate approach. It is possible to include with your publicity release a postcard stating as follows:

> If you wish to receive a complimentary copy of this publication for review purposes, please complete and return this postcard.

You will want to send releases to every publication that is targeted to your particular niche market. We also suggest that you send a release to all of the newspapers in your state or surrounding area. Editors are especially inclined to pick up releases from firms in your geographic region.

Do not overlook smaller newspapers and magazines. Small publications have limited staffs and are very likely to use well written material that is ready to print without editing. A number of small publications using your release can equal the circulation of one large publication.

Newsletters have become increasingly popular. One of the big advantages of newsletters is that they are often aimed at well-defined markets. We have enjoyed excellent sales whenever a newsletter mentions one of our books.

Your release should be addressed to a specific editor such as business book review editor, automotive book review editor, etc. Use the editor's name whenever possible.

Do not expect to receive immediate reviews or mentions of your book. Editors work several months in advance. Many months may pass before you receive your first "ink."

It is important to understand that a very high percent of your mailings will be nonproductive. However, you must also recognize that it only takes one "hit" with a large publication to fill your mail box with orders for several weeks. One of the greatest thrills of self-publishing is to go to the post office and find your box jammed with orders!

As compared to magazines, newspapers will provide more reviews than orders. However, the reviews may be viewed as ammunition for your promotional flyer sheets.

Magazines remain in circulation much longer than newspapers and will generate the greatest number of orders. If costs are a limiting factor, your best approach is to concentrate on magazines.

We suggest that you prepare a separate one page release for mailing to overseas publications in the English speaking world. Releases aimed at foreign publications should state that the postage and handling charges vary by country and all prices are in U.S. dollars.

For promotional purposes, you will want to obtain copies of every publication that mentions your book. Publishers will sometimes send you a copy of the publication carrying a review or reference to your book. By the same token, many publishers will not notify you when they give you publicity.

Frequently, you will open an envelope containing an order which will state "as mentioned in _____ magazine," please forward a copy of your book. In such cases, we send the person a complimentary copy and return the check with a request that they forward a copy of the publication mentioning our release. If you include a large preaddressed envelope, customers will nearly always forward the desired publication. If no response is received, you should purchase the publication or write to the editor and request a copy.

As a courtesy, we have often written to editors merely to thank them for publicity. It is always good to build a relationship with an editor who may help you with future releases.

Publicity is often referred to as being free which is not entirely correct. The costs involved in a simple publicity campaign include expenses relating to the following:

> printing a publicity release
> providing complimentary books
> purchasing a mailing list and/or publicity
>   directories
> purchasing shipping cartons and labels
> postage

It is frequently suggested that new self-publishers promote their books by participating in major trade shows and exhibits. We have found that participation in major trade shows is costly. Most of the trade shows are held in large cities where costs are high for hotels, meals and transportation. The cost of entering a trade show in itself is expensive and there is a strong likelihood that large publishers will dominate the event.

While trade shows are clearly advisable for established publishers, they are costly for a new venture. We believe that the monies can better be spent on an expanded publicity campaign with mailings to magazines, newspaper and newsletters with thousands of potential readers.

As a small publisher, you want to use every opportunity to demonstrate that you are a strong and growing firm. Beginning with your fifth year in business, we suggest that you publicize your anniversary every five years. For our fifteenth anniversary, we placed foil stickers on copies of all invoices, packing slips, etc. After ten years, we recommend that you begin using the phrase "publishing since _____."

During the year-end holiday season, we believe it is a good business practice to send your major customers a card expressing appreciation for their business. We suggest that you purchase a business oriented card with a simple message. In addition, we highly recommend that you add a personally written note such as "many thanks for your continued business — all best wishes."

With some exceptions, it is best not to send holiday gifts to valued customers. We once sent fruit baskets to a number of customers and promptly received stern letters advising us that it is against their policy for any employee to accept a holiday gift. Each year we receive numerous letters forbidding holiday gifts.

The importance of publicity cannot be overemphasized. Publicity is a bargain compared to the high cost of advertising. No other activity offers a greater return for small publishers than publicity.

XI
Advertising

MAGAZINE AND NEWSPAPER ADVERTISING

Advertising is very expensive for self-publishers. You will want to exhaust your best publicity efforts before taking on advertising.

A small ad in a national publication will normally cost thousands of dollars. With some publications, you can cut costs by placing your ad in regional editions. Nevertheless, you need to sell many books just to cover the cost of the placing an ad.

If you decide to advertise, we recommend that you initially place your ad in the leading publication aimed at your special market. Eventually, you will need to be cautious about advertising in markets where your book is in competition with catalog marketers. We once advertised in a leading publication directed at a niche market. We soon received a letter from the president of a large catalog customer wanting to know whether we were his supplier or competitor! In order not to offend the customer, we immediately stopped all ads in the industry's leading publication.

We are now very conscious of possible trade reaction to our advertising. In your early years, you can advertise anywhere and sell to anyone. As your business grows, your marketing strategies need to become more refined.

Based on our experience, the best months to advertise are September thru March. Book sales are especially strong during the year-end holiday season. In the winter months, people in the northern climate are more inclined to stay inside and read.

Because your ad will probably be small, it is important that you use a large headline in bold type. A small picture of the book should be included along with copy describing the best selling points. Be sure to include the price and complete ordering information.

A local typesetting firm can prepare your advertisement. You will want to compare typesetting costs because we have found large variances among different firms. When preparing an ad, always make sure that you provide the typesetter with the exact mechanical requirements of the publisher. If not prepared properly, publishers will sometimes tighten up or reduce your copy which can impair the ad's effectiveness.

By inserting a department number in the address, you will be able to determine the ad's success. Keep in mind that orders will be received months and sometimes years following the running of an ad.

DIRECT MAIL

We have experienced mixed results with direct mail. While we have lost money using some lists, we have made offsetting profit on other lists. Direct mail allows you to pinpoint your market. Large list brokers can provide you with potential buyers for virtually any subject. The minimum order is usually 5,000 names. You can purchase the names on pressure sensitive labels which can be directly affixed to your mailing piece.

The normal return rate on direct mail is one to two percent. If you send out 5,000 pieces, you can expect to receive between 50 and 100 responses.

Most experts recommend that you test a particular list before making a complete mailing. If you are unsuccessful with mailings to 1,000 addresses, you can cut your losses and terminate the mailings.

If your initial mailing is successful, you will want to maximize it to the fullest. Most brokers will provide sizeable discounts for large quantities. The success criteria is actually not the number of responses but the amount of profit generated. The profit realized from the returned orders must offset the cost of list rental, mailing piece, postage and labor. You must also recognize that some of the orders will result in repeat purchases and sales of other books.

We have had the best success with postcards which are relatively cheap to produce. Your local postmaster can assist you in determining the best and most economical means of mailing.

In every large mailing, a number of pieces will be returned by the post office for various reasons. Keep a record of the number of returned pieces because brokers will usually offer a credit whenever the quantity exceeds a specified level. Delivery of 99% of the names is often guaranteed.

By using different colored mailing pieces, you can evaluate the success of various mailing lists. We also keep track of the responses by state because some states seem to generate proportionately greater responses. For reasons unknown, we have enjoyed the best proportionate success with mailings to California.

We suggest that you buy the mailing list of subscribers to a magazine in your targeted market. If an individual is paying for a magazine, the chances are good that the address is current and correct.

It is recommended that you obtain addresses at places of employment rather than residences. In this highly mobile society, individuals are moving frequently and lists can quickly become obsolete. Employer addresses are less likely to change. For example, a mailing to an individual at a hospital will usually be delivered regardless of whether the individual remains employed. Another advantage of mailing to the place of employment is that many individuals will have their employer purchase the book.

We have found that direct mail is especially suitable during slow periods of business. Our mail order business generally slackens in the summer months. Direct mail helps keep employees busy and generates business when needed the most.

Neal Publications, Inc.
127 W. Indiana Ave. — P.O. Box 451
Perrysburg, Ohio 43552-0451
U.S.A.

NEED HELP
WITH
(PROBLEM)

IMPROVE YOUR
(SUBJECT)

WITH THIS
EFFECTIVE GUIDE

IT'S POWERFUL
AND

TIME PROVEN!

NP
Publishing Since 1978

SAMPLE DIRECT MAILING PIECE (FRONT SIDE)

ORDER TODAY!

(TITLE)

A Guide to
(DESCRIBE)

SIXTH EDITION

ISBN Number
LC Number
Number p.p.

(PUNCH LINE)
(STRESS BENEFITS)

$ 7.95 ea.
Plus Postage and Handling

Quantity discounts available
for 12 or more books
(419) 874-4787

(DETAILED DESCRIPTION
OF CONTENTS)

Please send _____ copy(ies) of

(TITLE)   = $_____

(Ohio residents add sales tax)

Plus $_____ each for Shipping
and Handling   = $_____

Enclosed is a check or
money order in U.S. funds
for the total amount of $_____

SHIPPING and HANDLING	
1 Book	$2.00
2 Books	Each 1.25
3-5 Books	Each 1.00
6-11 Books	Each .50
12 or More (U.S.)	No Charge

MOST
ORDERS
SHIPPED
WITHIN
24 HOURS
OF RECEIPT

Send Orders to:
NEAL PUBLICATIONS, INC.
127 W. Indiana Ave. P.O. Box 451
Perrysburg, Ohio 43552-0451
U.S.A.

Name _____
Address _____
City _____ State _____
Phone _____ Zip _____

SAMPLE DIRECT MAILING PIECE (REVERSE SIDE)

51

XII
Creating an Order Form

A well designed order form will produce business and reduce the need for follow-up telephone calls and correspondence. The form should include a picture of the book along with the following:

> brief description of book
> number of pages
> prices in U.S. Dollars including postage
>   and handling
> shipping and handling charges
> ISBN number
> Library of Congress number
> request for action

We suggest that you include the statement "prices subject to change without notice." You will be receiving order forms for many years and you want to cover yourself with regard to price changes.

It is suggested that you make the space for the name and address as large as possible. Handwriting is often difficult to read and providing a large space will reduce errors and help avoid the need for follow-up clarifications.

The listing of a toll free number is normally recommended. However, we have found that professional books are usually purchased by persons calling at the expense of their employers who often qualify for volume rates. We very seldom receive requests for toll free numbers and we have never accepted collect calls. Whether you should incur the added expense of a toll free number depends on your field of speciality and your type of customers.

After using many versions, we have experienced the greatest success with the order form shown below:

------- ORDER TODAY ! -------

NEAL PUBLICATIONS, INC.
127 W. Indiana Ave. P.O. Box 451
Perrysburg, Ohio 43552-0451
U.S.A.

(419) 874-4787
Please send the book(s) requested.

SHIPPING AND HANDLING (Covers Any Combination)	
1 Book	$2.00
2 Books	Each 1.25
3-5 Books	Each 1.00
6-11 Books	Each .50
12 or More (U.S.)	No Charge

_____copy(ies) (TITLE)
$7.95 each $_____

_____copy(ies) (TITLE)
$5.95 each $_____

_____copy(ies) (TITLE)
$7.95 each $_____

_____copy(ies) (TITLE)
$4.95 each $_____

⇨ ⇨ Plus $_____ Each
for Shipping and Handling $ _____

Total (U.S. Funds) $ _____

Name _____

Address _____

City _____ State _____ Zip _____

Ohio residents add sales tax — Quantity discounts available on order for twelve or more — Prices subject to change without notice

SAMPLE ORDER FORM

Order forms should be shipped with all books and included with requests for literature.

When order forms are sent overseas, we place a large "X" over the shipping and handling section while noting that "overseas rates vary."

Although it is common practice among large publishers, we have found it best not to include a printed order form in the book itself. Booksellers and especially catalog merchandisers want to consider you as a supplier, not a competitor.

You will also need a different order form for internal use. The form should be very spacious because people placing orders by telephone often talk very fast and you need plenty of room for addresses which include titles, buildings, suites, mail stops, etc. Be sure to include space for a purchase order number because you may not receive payment without it. Many years of experience have taught us that you also want to repeat the shipping address to the caller to ensure its accuracy.

XIII
Preparing Promotional
Flyer Sheets

Attractive flyer sheets promoting a book are vital to your selling efforts.

If you are selling several books, we recommend a separate flyer sheet for each publication. Each sheet should be a different color to stimulate interest. Keep in mind that black ink on yellow paper is one of the most eye catching color combinations. You will want to use a relatively light-weight paper in order to reduce postal costs.

The flyer sheet should basically include the same information as the order form. You will want to include the price, shipping and handling charges, ISBN number, Library of Congress number and the number of pages. Use the words "new," "latest," or "expanded edition" at every opportunity because they convey a strong message.

In comparison with an order form, the flyer sheet should describe the book in greater detail with powerful headlines. The flyer sheet should also include any reviews or excerpts from reviews quoting the exact wording. If you are fortunate to receive a number of reviews, we recommend that they be printed on a separate sheet.

Be sure your flyer sheet requests action such as "ORDER TODAY."

Whenever information is requested, it is advisable to send one or more flyer sheets plus your order form. The same materials should be included in each book that is sold to individuals. If several books are shipped to a single address, we recommend that literature be enclosed in each book. Several books in one shipment will be redistributed and your literature should accompany each book. When sending a number of books to a reseller, it is only necessary to include one complete set of literature.

During the year-end holiday season, books are very popular gifts. You want to remind your customers that your publication would make a perfect gift.

In the middle of October, we begin packing our books with the following bookmark:

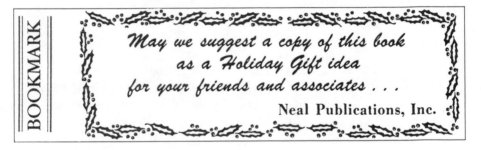

SAMPLE HOLIDAY BOOKMARK

In the mail order business, flyer sheets and other enclosures are your silent salespersons. Make sure all your printed materials are colorful, attention getting and effective.

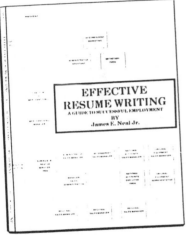
SAMPLE FLYER SHEET

EFFECTIVE LETTERS FOR BUSINESS, PROFESSIONAL AND PERSONAL USE
A GUIDE TO SUCCESSFUL CORRESPONDENCE

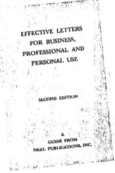

ISBN 1-882423-00-3
LC 93-92688

ONLY

$6⁹⁵ each

Plus $2.00 for Postage and Handling

Quantity Discounts Available

With This New Guide, You Can Quickly Prepare Effective Letters That Will Convey Warmth and Friendship.

Each Letter is Designed To Allow The Broadest Possible Use. Makes Letter Writing Fast, Easy and Professional!

Contains Over 150 Time-Tested Letters To Meet a Wide Variety of Correspondence Needs . . . Order Today!

Table of Contents
LETTERS OF:

ACCEPTANCE	CONFIRMATION	INTRODUCTION	REQUEST
ACKNOWLEDGEMENT	CONGRATULATION	INVITATION	RESIGNATION
ANNOUNCEMENT	CONGRESSIONAL MEMBER	PRICE INCREASE	RESUME
APOLOGY	CRITICISM	PRODUCT CHANGE	SALES
APPLICATION	CUSTOMER GOODWILL	PURCHASE ORDER	SOLICITATION
APPRECIATION	DONATION	RECOMMENDATION	SYMPATHY
CANCELLATION	FAREWELL	REFUSAL	TERMINATION
COLLECTION	HOLIDAY GREETING	RENT	WELCOME
COMPLAINT	ILLNESS	REPORTING A SUCCESS	

NEAL PUBLICATIONS, INC.
127 W. Indiana Ave. - P. O. Box 451
Perrysburg, OH 43552-0451 U.S.A.

SAMPLE FLYER SHEET

58

XIV
Producing A Catalog

When you offer only a single book, a flyer sheet is basically your catalog. As soon as you have two or more books in your line, you will need a catalog.

The cover of a catalog should include the name of your company along with a powerful punch line.

Your catalog listing should contain an actual picture of the book with a brief description of the contents. The listing should include the following:

> ISBN Number
> Library of Congress Catalog Number
> Number of pages
> Price
> Shipping and Handling Charges
> Order Form

General ordering and shipping information and other items and conditions such as applicable taxes should be listed in a separate section. Be sure to stimulate action and request an order.

A catalog is your silent salesperson. Be sure your catalog is attractive and distribute it freely.

Achieve a richer,

more rewarding career

with these powerful

self-help guides from

Publishing Since 1978

Neal Publications, Inc.

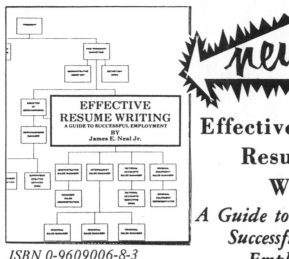

Effective Resume Writing

A Guide to Successful Employment

ISBN 0-9609006-8-3
LC 90-063084
104 p.p.

$ 7.95 ea.

Plus Postage and Handling

Provides strategic insights and practical advice for achieving job hunting success.

Table of Contents

This guide is packed with the key elements needed to write a powerful resume. It is a no-nonsense down-to-earth guide for preparing effective resumes and transmittal letters. Covers all phases of job hunting. Shows how to present yourself, attract attention and get results!

Quantity discounts available
for 12 or more books.

Call: (419) 874-4787

SAMPLE CATALOG BOOK LISTING

ORDERING AND SHIPPING INFORMATION

WE SHIP MOST ORDERS WITHIN 48 HOURS OF RECEIPT

FOUR OR MORE PUBLICATIONS ARE SHIPPED BY U.P.S. IN THE U.S., EXCLUDING ALASKA AND HAWAII

SPECIAL RATES APPLY TO NEXT DAY AIR, SECOND DAY AIR, CANADA AND OVERSEAS SHIPMENTS

SHIPMENTS TO APO ADDRESSES ARE BY PARCEL POST

SEE ORDER FORM FOR SHIPPING AND HANDLING CHARGES

ALL SHIPPING AND HANDLING CHARGES APPLY TO A SINGLE SHIPMENT TO A SINGLE ADDRESS

SIZEABLE QUANTITY DISCOUNTS ARE AVAILABLE

OHIO RESIDENTS ADD SALES TAX

PRICES ARE SUBJECT TO CHANGE WITHOUT NOTICE

ALL PUBLICATIONS ARE PRINTED
WITH PRIDE
IN THE UNITED STATES OF AMERICA

NEAL PUBLICATIONS, INC.
127 W. Indiana Ave. — P. O. Box 451
Perrysburg, Ohio 43552 - 0451, U.S.A.

SAMPLE OF ORDERING AND SHIPPING SECTION

XV
Selling

Sales are the lifeblood of your business. You may be intellectual, highly educated and a brilliant writer but nothing will happen without sales.

Telephone selling is becoming very important in today's marketplace. Your business phone should be promptly answered in a cheerful and enthusiastic tone. Additional sales can often be obtained by pointing out the lower handling and shipping costs that apply to larger orders. Whenever a person places an order for a single book, always mention that the shipping and handling charges will be less for two books.

Niche marketing offers great opportunities for sales of related books. As your line expands, you can tactfully suggest that the caller may also be interested in buying another book on a similar subject.

One of the big advantages of book selling is that you have potential customers everywhere. In addition to printed messages, you need to personally promote your book at every opportunity.

Be sure to have your business cards with you at all times. Take a copy of your book whenever you travel. You never know who you will meet.

I once met an army sergeant while sipping a beverage in Las Vegas. He expressed interest in my business and I later sent him a complimentary copy of one of our books. He apparently reviewed the book with others because we soon began to receive many orders from his military base.

As another example, my wife once gave a complimentary book to a bookseller located close to one of the nation's largest medical centers. As a result of one complimentary copy, we received orders for hundreds of books.

You need to be enthusiastic and never stop selling!

XVI
Pricing, Terms, Compliances, Receivables and Returns

PRICING AND TERMS

Establishing a price for your book is one of your most critical decisions. It has always been our belief that most successful self-publishers offer low-priced books preferably under $10.00. You want to price your book to sell at about one-half the price of similar titles published by the major houses.

Arriving at a price depends on a number of circumstances. Are you running your business from your kitchen table? Are you going to rent an office? Are you going to run the business yourself or do you plan to hire someone? In order to arrive at an initial price, we suggest that you multiply the cost of your book by six or seven times.

In general, set your price higher rather than lower. You are going to have an investment in materials with a printed price. Changing prices at a later date is costly.

Some of the unplanned costs which can happen (and usually will) are as follows:

> higher packaging costs
> increased postal rates
> increased private carrier rates
> higher federal, state and local taxes
> higher license renewal fees
> higher tax preparation fees

increased rent
increased insurance costs
higher utility costs

You can increase your sales by offering quantity discounts. We suggest discount breaks of 2, 6, 12, 24, or more.

We recommend that pricing structures include a shipping and handling charge especially on smaller orders. If you review the catalogs of many mail order firms, you will find significant differences in shipping and handling policies. Some firms charge a flat shipping and handling fee regardless of the size of the order. Other companies apply a handling charge based on the dollar value or weight of shipment.

The policy that we have found successful is to apply a descending handling and shipping charge with no fee for shipments of twelve or more books.

By using a scale of decreasing handling and shipping fees, you will encourage buyers to order larger quantities. I would estimate that 90% of our customers who call by phone and plan to order five books will increase their order to six copies when they learn of the lower handling and shipping charge. Persons placing orders of 11 books will nearly always increase their order to 12 in order to eliminate shipping and handling charges.

We have found it advisable not to initially include a price on your book. By not having a printed price, you are in a better position to change prices. You will need to establish a suggested price for resellers.

Major distributors expect to receive a 50% discount from your suggested price while bookstores expect a 30 to 40% discount. They also expect terms of net 90. However, we have found that shorter payment terms are possible when strictly enforced and the book is unique.

We suggest that you give public libraries a discount of

20%. Many people will order your book after seeing it in a library.

Catalog houses will usually require a contract guaranteeing a price for a year or longer. Price changes need to be coordinated with existing contracts. As a general rule, price changes should become effective on January 1 and July 1. Whenever a decision is made to change prices, you should give your wholesale customers as much advance notice as possible.

In situations where a new customer orders a large quantity of books, we require at least a one-half advance payment. We will frequently receive a phone call similar to the following:

> This is the _____ bookstore calling. We wish to place an order for 200 copies of _____. Our purchase order no. is and our shipping and billing address is _____.

It is always amazing how some small firms believe they can simply pick up the phone as a first time customer and order hundreds of dollars of books while expecting to be billed. As a new business, you need to protect yourself and insist on an advance payment of one-half or more. Since most large orders are from a retailer who has received a special order, you will nearly always receive the advance payment without any problems.

GOVERNMENT COMPLIANCE REQUESTS

Whenever you sell to large organizations, you will often receive requests for all types of information relating to your business. You will be requested to provide information such as the following:

Federal Employer Identification Number
Social Security Number
Fair Employment Practices
Number of Employees

Classification of Local Labor Market
Annual Sales
Size of Warehouse
Country of Manufacture
Contract Price or Open Market
Drug Free Workplace

Although you may believe that this information is confidential, you need to promptly comply with all reasonable requests. Corporations and government agencies at the federal, state and local levels will simply not issue a check without first receiving a variety of completed forms. Sometimes it is necessary to complete several forms and return them at your expense in order to receive payment for a single book!

RECEIVABLES

You need to place a high priority on continuously monitoring your accounts receivables. Our Company has terms of 30 days net. If an invoice is unpaid after 45 days, we send a copy of the invoice to the customer with a "friendly reminder — your account is overdue" sticker. If invoices are unpaid after 60 days, we send another copy of the invoice with a sterner message. After 75 days, we sent a certified letter which is usually successful. Telephone calls are also made especially to businesses.

When customers become 60 days overdue, we enter the account into our "red" file. Once an account is flagged, they are placed on a "cash with order" basis only.

Although we sometimes remove an account from our "red" file, they will usually soon return to the "cash with order" only status. It seems that some companies pay late as a matter of routine policy.

It is important that you have your "red" file either in a manual or computer data base close to your order desk. Accounts who have been on a "cash with order" basis for years will continue to call and place routine orders. They must be promptly told that advance payment is necessary. Most of the "red file" accounts will send advance payment because they wish to honor a special order with one of their customers.

It takes discipline to maintain a close watch on your accounts receivables. Yet, sound business practice requires close attention to the monies owed to you.

RETURNS

Every business has unique problems. In publishing, returns are always a concern. With sound policies, you can restrict returns to reasonable numbers. We have a long standing policy of limiting returns to the current edition of any book plus a six month grace period. You simply cannot accept the return of books that are out of print. We also require prior approval before accepting returns.

It is important to closely adhere to your return policy. Individual retail stores of large marketers will often purchase one book. Although the quantity of books shipped to a single outlet may not be large, the potential for returns from hundreds of outlets is significant. We have found that companies will often return books that are five or six years old and take an automatic credit from their outstanding invoices.

Always inspect each returned book. In addition to refusing credit for old books, you cannot accept books that are damaged and not resaleable. Bookstores will often affix all kinds of stickers and mark returned copies. Some of the books returned to us have been in deplorable condition.

We recommend that you issue a credit memo or a check for the cost of the publication only. Transportation charges on returned books should be paid by the buyer with no credit given for any handling charges.

You need to limit your liability for returns and the best

method is to provide marketers with a clearly defined written policy.

ADHERENCE TO POLICY

Over the years, we have learned that it is essential to develop written policies concerning your prices, terms and other conditions. Customers will aggressively seek better prices and other conditions.

Be careful not to make concessions. Once you start to make exceptions, you create a tangled web that will only lead to problems.

For example, assume you give a special price or other condition to one account based on some weak justification. Eventually, the account is purchased by a larger account who has not been given special consideration. You have placed yourself in an untenable position.

We have lost considerable business because we would not deviate from one of our established policies. In the long-run, we have created a solid reputation for integrity which is worth more than a short-term loss of business. Beginning with your first customer, strive to build a good reputation that will give your company a strong foundation for future growth.

XVII
Packaging and Shipping

Fast order processing and prompt shipments are strong factors in promoting repeat sales. Customers are more likely to place repeat orders when prompt delivery is previously experienced.

As a small firm, you can provide faster service than the large publishing companies. You want to capitalize on this advantage to the fullest. Our firm ships approximately 95% of all orders on the same day that they are received!

Orders sent by mail on Thursday and Friday will normally be received on the following Monday making it the busiest day of the week. Incoming mail is usually the lowest on Tuesdays and gradually builds until the following Tuesday. Orders tend to decrease in the days before and after a national holiday.

You will want customers to receive your books in perfect condition with no bends, scratches or dog-eared covers. We suggest that you briefly inspect each book prior to packaging. We have found that about 90% of defects involve either the front or back covers along with the first and last pages. Although padded envelopes are cheaper, we believe that cardboard boxes are the best containers.

One of the best cost saving measures is to request that your printer supply books in cartons of 50 or 25 depending on their weight and size. For quantity orders, it is possible to reuse the original cartons for shipment to your customers.

Another cost saving measure is to save all the packing

materials that are packed with your supplies. Nearly all packaging materials can be reused in shipping your books.

We have had excellent success by wrapping books in 3/8″ bubbled plastic before inserting them into a cardboard carton. In addition to protecting the books, plastic conveys the image that you are quality conscious and adds to the perceived value.

As mentioned previously, each shipment should contain literature and a repeat order form.

With each shipment, we also suggest that you include a "thank you" card similar to the following:

Neal Publications, Inc. 127 W. Indiana Ave. – P.O. Box 451 Perrysburg, Ohio 43552-0451, U.S.A.	**Neal Publications, Inc.** 127 W. Indiana Ave. – P.O. Box 451 Perrysburg, Ohio 43552-0451, U.S.A.
Thank you for your order. **We sincerely hope you find the publication to be helpful.** **Your purchase is appreciated and we look forward to serving you again.** **Neal Publications, Inc.**	**Thank you for your order.** **Your purchase is appreciated and we look forward to serving you again.** **Neal Publications, Inc.**
SAMPLE THANK YOU CARD NON-BOOKSELLER	SAMPLE THANK YOU CARD BOOKSELLER

When responding to requests for information, we recommend that you enclose with your literature a separate card such as the example shown below:

Neal
Publications, Inc.
127 W. Indiana Ave. — P.O. Box 451
Perrysburg, Ohio 43552-0451, U.S.A.

Thank you for your inquiry.

We are pleased to enclose the ordering information which you requested.

Your interest is very much appreciated and we look forward to receiving your order.

Neal Publications, Inc.

SAMPLE ACKNOWLEDGEMENT CARD

Invoices to an individual for a single book may be packed in the book itself so that the word "invoice" overlaps the cover. Invoices to an organization should be placed outside the carton in a bright "invoice enclosed" envelope or sent directly to the customer's accounts payable department.

Packing slips to individuals may be placed inside the book with the "packing slip" heading overlapping the cover. For organizations and businesses, the packing slip should be placed outside the carton in an envelope marked "packing slip enclosed."

Book wholesalers and retailers will frequently request drop shipments to their customers. Drop shipments require special handling. Never include promotional literature or pricing information with a drop shipment. Remember that the person receiving the book is not your customer and he or she may be paying a retail price which differs from your suggested resale price. Include only a packing slip with drop shipments.

For orders up to three books, we suggest that you send them via the U.S. Postal Service marked "Special Fourth Class." Books enjoy a special lower postal rate and you want to make the most of this benefit. It should be noted, however, that you cannot trace regular and uninsured fourth class mail.

For orders of four or more books depending on the weight and price, we recommend shipment by a private carrier. Parcel carrier rates are higher but they are automatically insured up to a stated value and tracing is quick and easy.

Shipments to overseas customers require special attention. We frequently receive purchase orders from overseas buyers marked "ship via air mail" without enclosing sufficient postage. Air mail postage is costly and varies widely by country. Before shipping overseas, you need to determine the exact postage by using a Postal Service rate chart or obtaining the fee from the post office. We normally provide the customer with a price quote including shipment by surface and air mail. You should be aware that surface shipments may take several months to arrive at some destinations. We use the Postal Service for all overseas shipments because the fees of private carriers are too costly.

We highly recommend that you insure all overseas shipments because we have experienced many situations where the customer will advise that the shipment was never received. You are less likely to encounter shipping difficulties with insured packages.

We suggest "special fourth class" mail for all shipments to Alaska, Hawaii, and Canada.

Shipments to members of the armed forces using an AE box may be sent at the special fourth class mail rate. However, special custom forms must be attached to the outside of all cartons destined for shipment overseas and to Canada.

You should be aware that a number of firms offer fulfillment services. After a book comes off the press, it is possible to transfer all operational functions to an outside company. They will accept orders, ship your book and bill customers. A fulfillment service will provide you with a monthly summary of transactions. The problem with fulfillment services is that they will siphon off a large percent of the profits. If you are smart enough to write a fast selling book, you are surely capable of providing the business functions needed to achieve maximum profits.

XVIII
Keeping Records

Accurate record keeping is essential to your business success. You need accurate records for the following reasons:

1. preparing federal, state and local tax returns
2. tracking sales
3. analyzing costs
4. monitoring accounts receivables and accounts payable
5. controlling inventories
6. preparing financial statements

Whether you keep computer or handwritten records, discipline is critical. Some people do their bookkeeping on a daily basis while others set aside a certain day for this important function.

Although many standard computer programs are available, we have found that a personalized system is best. Our firm uses a personalized program prepared by an expert. The personalized system has increased our efficiency throughout the company. For example, invoices are prepared by merely entering the name, shipping and billing addresses, date and the number of ordered books by title that are ordered. The computers automatically prepare prices, appropriate handling fees and taxes where applicable. Computers have dramatically increased our operating efficiency while allowing us to reduce labor costs.

INVOICES

Our computers prepare invoices with five copies which are distributed as follows:

original and first copy .... to customer
second and third copies........ to accounts receivable
packing slip .... sent with shipment

The second and third copies of the invoice are stapled to the original order and envelope. All outstanding documents are filed in a tub with hanging folders.

Be careful to never send an invoice with a drop shipment. Many times a bookseller will request that shipment be made directly to their customer. You do not want the customer to know the seller's purchase price.

PACKING SLIPS

Packing slips require one original and one copy. The original is sent with the shipment and the remaining copy is retained with the order. For cash sales, we stamp the packing slip "PAID" along with the date and amount. Packing slips should always be included with shipments to businesses and other organizations. A packing slip without any pricing information should accompany all drop shipments.

A good rule is to always prepare a packing slip whenever you receive a purchase order number. A copy of the packing slip along with the order is placed in the original envelope and filed by date.

ACCOUNTS RECEIVABLE

Accurate records are vital to monitoring your accounts receivables. You need to know which accounts are 30, 60, and 90 days overdue. You also want to track your total receivables.

INVENTORY CONTROL

It is critical to closely follow your book and packaging inventories. Books cannot be quickly printed. You may have to wait 60 to 90 days for delivery. We have found that the best approach is to establish a predetermined ordering level allowing ample lead time.

Accurate inventory records will greatly assist you in preparing financial statements and tax returns. Your inventories should be at their lowest level on the date specified for determining inventory or business property taxes.

CHECKING ACCOUNT

We suggest that you establish a separate checking account for your business expenditures. It's sound business practice to write a check rather than paying cash for most business expenses.

ACCOUNTS PAYABLE

As a start-up business, it is critical that you pay your bills on time and keep all accounts current. As a growing business, you will require more and more supplies. New suppliers will often request the names and addresses of your other suppliers. You want to be in a position where you will gladly give the names of other suppliers who have received your prompt payments. You will be amazed how fast the national credit rating companies will develop a profile on your business.

EXPENSES

Beginning with your very first expenditure, you need to record and retain all receipts. We suggest that you break down all expenses by unit. If you purchase 24 rolls of packaging tape at a total cost of $48.00, you should record the unit cost at $2.00 each. Recording unit cost will make it much easier to assign dollar values when it comes time to taking your annual inventory.

SALES

Each large customer should be assigned an account number. You will want to continuously monitor your sales by customer. Sales information by customer is especially needed when catalog marketers request that you participate in a cooperative advertising program. You need to make sure that you are not offering more co-op monies than the customer is entitled.

We recommend that sales records be maintained by the month and year to date. Over a period of time, sales records have proven to be our best guide and business barometer.

Make sure you have backup files for all your records. We believe it is advisable to keep your original records at the office and store backup disks and reports at your home. If you operate your business from your home, you should maintain duplicate records in different areas of the house or preferably in another location. Storing vital records at two locations will avoid any problems due to a fire or other catastrophe.

XIX
Achieving and
Maintaining Profitability

It may be several years before your business generates steady profits. Profitability can be achieved faster by keeping your overhead down. Remember the old saying "if you take care of the pennies, the dollars will take care of themselves." Try to keep a tight lid on costs while investing in areas that will make your business grow.

As soon as profits begin to materialize, many small business owners cannot resist the temptation to spend money. You can easily reduce or eliminate your profits by:

> hiring too many employees
> joining many industry associations
> attending many distant seminars
> subscribing to numerous publications
> sending numerous fax transmissions overseas
> making extensive use of mobile phones
> hiring a telephone answering service
> hiring custodian and landscape services
> contributing to many community and charitable
> programs.

You need to realize that over a period of several years, cost inflation will creep into your business.

A small annual increase in a private carrier's shipping rates may not seem significant. However, rate increases over several years will greatly increase your shipping costs. As a result, your shipping and handling charges must be periodically reviewed.

The cost of a second printing may reflect higher paper charges amounting to only several cents a book. The accumulated cost increases covering several reprintings may be significant. Book prices must continuously be evaluated in light of ever rising costs.

Over a period of time, the combination of higher manufacturing, shipping and marketing costs can be devastating to your profitability. It is critical that your prices keep pace with increasing costs.

We believe quite strongly that the two best approaches to making big profits in self-publishing are heavy emphasis on marketing (advertising, distribution, sales promotion and selling) along with keeping your labor costs low. In particular, payroll costs can be a tremendous burden when you consider all the applicable federal, state and local taxes. As an employer, you can also expect numerous other costs such as health premiums, workers' compensation, unemployment services, school taxes, etc. You simply must resist the temptation to hire additional employees. If you are willing to work long hours, you can keep your payroll costs down and significantly build your net worth.

XX
Adding Books From Other Publishers

In an earlier chapter, we noted that niche marketing is the key to success in self-publishing. One of the best means of expanding within your niche is to add similar books.

As sales of your book increase, you will have all the systems in place to add other publications. Personal computers can easily be programmed to add titles. Your shipping area can handle more books by merely purchasing a variety of carton sizes. You should also be able to add books without increasing the number of employees.

In order to select suitable titles, you will want to scan the catalog and directory files at major libraries and bookstores. Select titles which will complement your own books in both quality and price. Be sure that the additional books will enhance your overall line.

Your next step is to contact the publisher and attempt to purchase the desired book at up to 50% off the retail price. Large publishers will usually refer you to a large wholesaler but smaller firms will often sell directly to you. If referred to a wholesaler, contact a firm which already buys books from you. They will probably have an outstanding balance with you which increases your negotiating position.

Once you start selling a book from another publisher, it is critical that you closely monitor inventories. Books can quickly go out of print and you do not want to get yourself in a position where you are receiving orders for a title that is no longer available. You can maintain smaller inventories of the books which you publish because you are in complete control. We have found it advisable to maintain a six month's stock of all titles purchased on the open market.

Rather than incorporate the new book into your own literature, we suggest that you prepare a separate flyer sheet with an order form. If a new book does not sell, you can simply discard the separate flyer sheet without affecting your other literature. The technique is similar to receiving a bill in the mail with many other items offered for sale.

When preparing a flyer sheet for a book which you have purchased on the open market, we suggest that you state the name of the publisher in your literature. As a publisher, you do not want to misrepresent your company by implying that you publish all the books which you offer for sale.

We have found that sales of more than one book can be extremely profitable. Packaging and postal charges will increase by about 30% when you sell two books to one customer instead of one.

Perhaps of greater importance, adding books enhances the image of your business. A broader line makes your firm appear larger, stronger and more reliable.

Customers who place orders on the telephone often inquire about other books which are available in the same general field. For example, a person ordering a book on resumes, will often ask if other books are available on cover letters, interviewing, etc.

In cases when a customer does not inquire about other books, it is very easy for the person in the order department to say "perhaps you would be interested in other excellent books which we offer such as _____."

In large companies, purchase orders are usually required. Some purchase orders for a single book may consist of a number of pages. If a customer is required to take the time and effort to complete a purchase requisition, obtain budget numbers, etc., there is a strong tendency to expand the number of books ordered.

Selling books from other publishers allows you to offer a full service line and greatly add to your profits!

XXI
Special Problems and Solutions

A big advantage of self-publishing is that you can provide the type of excellence in customer service that cannot be matched by large firms. You do not have to deal with bureaucracies, committees and all kinds of rules and regulations. You should maximize your competitive edge in providing superior customer service.

Despite your best plans, policies and procedures, a number of situations will occur that require special handling. You can expect the following:

CUSTOMER FORWARDS OVERPAYMENT

When overpayment is received, you will want to make a refund. If your total price is $9.95, for example, many customers will forward a check for $10.00. We recommend that you enclose with the shipment a .05 cash refund. If the refund is several dollars or more, we suggest that you return a check separately.

CUSTOMER FORWARDS UNDERPAYMENT

In cases where a customer's payment is short by .50 or less, it is suggested that you accept the payment with no further action. The cost of an envelope, notice and postage will be greater than the additional amount due. For underpayments of above .50, we send a request for the additional amount due. If you enclose a preaddressed and postage paid envelope, we have found that the response rate will be very high.

CUSTOMER FORWARDS CREDIT CARD NUMBER WHICH YOU DO NOT ACCEPT

In order to reduce costs, our firm has never accepted credit cards. If a person requests that we charge a book to a credit card, we ship the book with an invoice stating "Since we do not accept credit cards, we are shipping the requested book(s) with this invoice. We trust our handling will be satisfactory." To our knowledge, we have never lost a single order because we do not accept credit cards. In fact, customers are very impressed that we trust them. Moreover, our bad debts have always been very low.

It should be noted, however, that customers who provide you with a credit card number will assume that the book is paid in full. Invoices sent to a person who requested a credit card charge should clearly state that credit cards are not accepted. Invoices of this type require close follow-up.

CUSTOMER FORWARDS A CHECK ONLY WITH NO RECORD OF AN ORDER OR INVOICE

Frequently, we receive checks without any reference to an order or invoice. If we are unable to locate an invoice, we make a copy of the check before depositing it. Large companies will sometimes send a subsequent order within a couple of weeks. If no clarification is received after two weeks, we forward a copy of the check to the individual or the sender's accounts payable department with a request for additional information.

CUSTOMER REFUSES TO PAY HANDLING CHARGE

Sometimes booksellers will order one or two books and refuse to pay a handling charge. You must treat all customers equally and require all accounts to do business on your terms and conditions. Accounts who will not accept your conditions should be referred to a distributor.

CUSTOMER ADVISES THAT THE ORDERED
BOOK WAS NEVER RECEIVED

A customer will sometimes notify you that a book was never received. It is important that you check your records to verify that the order was received and shipped. In many cases, you will find that the order was never received and the customer should be advised. If the book was shipped and a reasonable shipping period has elapsed, you will immediately want to ship another book with a packing slip marked "DUPLICATE SHIPMENT."

CUSTOMER ADVISES THAT THE
WRONG BOOK WAS SHIPPED

If your line consists of several or more books, you will invariably ship the wrong title from time to time. Whenever a customer informs us that another low-priced book was shipped in place of the title ordered, we immediately ship the proper book and advise the customer to keep the book received with our compliments.

CUSTOMER ADVISES OF A SHORT SHIPMENT

Whenever a customer advises that a shipment was incomplete, we immediately ship an additional book or two with a note saying that we are sorry for the inconvenience. On large orders, we check our carrier shipping records which will indicate the weight within a fraction of an ounce. If we have proof of delivery and the weight is correct, we will refuse to send additional books. Of course, if the weight is not correct, we will immediately ship additional copies.

CUSTOMER ADVISES OF DEFECTIVE BOOKS

Although we have had few complaints, the most common quality problem is pages missing. We have experienced missing pages with many different printers. If only one or two books are reported as defective, we immediately ship replacements with a note expressing our regret. If larger quantities are reported as defective, we request a return shipment before making replacement.

CUSTOMER'S ADDRESS IS CONFUSING OR ILLEGIBLE

It is not uncommon to receive an order which does not clearly show the customer's address. In this mobile society, different addresses often appear on the envelope, order form and bank check. As a general rule, it's best to use the handwritten address. We suggest that you purchase a copy of the National Five-Digit Zip Code & Post Office Directory published by the U.S. Postal Service. The directory lists all zip code numbers and provides a description of street numbers for major cities and suburbs.

CUSTOMER ORDERS BOOKS
FOR A LARGE ORGANIZATION
WITHOUT A PURCHASE ORDER NUMBER

Persons will often order a quantity of books and request that the invoice be sent to their accounts payable department. Accounting departments will not normally issue a check without a corresponding purchase order number. Individuals requesting books from a large firm should be advised that a purchase order number is required. Without a purchase order number, you may spend months trying to receive payment.

BANK RETURNS CUSTOMER CHECK

Occasionally, your bank will return a check marked "INSUFFICIENT FUNDS" or "ACCOUNT CLOSED." Upon receiving a returned check, it is essential that you promptly send a copy of the check to the person advising that immediate payment is required. We recommend a certified letter with a return receipt requested.

FOREIGN ORDERS ARE RECEIVED WITHOUT SPECIFYING METHOD OF SHIPMENT

We have encountered many situations where foreign customers do not request a method of shipment. If you ship books by surface, they may take a couple of months to arrive. In the meantime, the customer is calling by phone or sending a fax to request a duplicate shipment. It is best to ship books overseas by air. However, air shipments are costly. We also recommend that you insure most overseas shipments which tends to ensure delivery. In short, you should always clarify the method of shipping overseas with the customer prior to mailing.

PAYMENT IS NOT IN U.S. DOLLARS

Despite an invoice clearly marked U.S. dollars, we have received many checks from foreign firms that are not in U.S. dollars. Depending on the country, the currency difference can be significant especially on a large order. In such cases, we return the check requesting payment in U.S. dollars.

BANK WILL NOT ACCEPT FOREIGN CHECKS

Many banks will not accept foreign checks even when drawn in U.S. dollars. In such cases, you will need to open an account in a bank which maintains a foreign currency department.

GOVERNMENT ORDERS DO NOT INCLUDE SHIPPING AND HANDLING CHARGES

Orders from federal, state and local governments require special scrutiny. In particular, the federal government often fails to allow for shipping and handling charges. If the order lists a price of $7.95 F.O.B. Destination and you bill $7.95 plus $2.00 for shipping and handling, you will receive a check for $7.95 with no recourse. In such cases, you want to make a copy of the incoming order for your files and return the original with a request for an amended order to cover shipping and handling.

REQUESTS FOR COMPLIMENTARY COPIES

Many persons contact small publishers and request complimentary books. It's best to limit complimentary copies to reviewers, college professors, instructors and persons with the authority to purchase large quantities of books. In our business, the most frequent request is from academic people who ask for "desk copies." It is customary to provide an instructor with a complimentary "desk copy" only in situations where students are required to purchase your book. We suggest that you use discretion in providing complimentary copies.

XXII
Targeting for Success

Success in self-publishing cannot be achieved in a short time. It takes years of dedication and hard work to make a publishing business prosper.

Yet, self-publishing offers tremendous opportunities. The success of a single book can change your lifestyle forever.

The thrill of receiving your first orders is an experience that you will never forget.

As you develop distribution, sales will grow and grow. Eventually, you will want to write a second book.

With self-publishing, you can truly turn a nominal investment into a fortune.

We wish you ever success!

Action Plan for Success

SUBJECT SELECTION

1. Select a subject that you know.

2. Choose a subject which is resistant to change.

3. Give priority consideration to writing a "How To" book.

4. Read extensively on your chosen subject.

TITLE SELECTION

5. Select a title that is self-explanatory.

6. Consider a subtitle if greater clarification is needed.

7. Conduct a search to make certain that your chosen title does not currently exist.

MANUSCRIPT

8. Become knowledgeable on publishing laws.

9. Use small words and write concisely.

10. Purchase a good stylebook for reference.

11. Seek opinions from trusted friends on your manuscript.

12. Use a professional typesetter who specializes in books.

13. Be sure to thoroughly proofread your manuscript.

14. Consider an outside proofreader.

MARKETING STRATEGY

15. Develop a marketing plan.

16. Concentrate on a niche market.

17. Plan to eventually offer a line of books within your marketing niche.

18. Attempt to establish a broad customer base.

19. Seek distribution by contacting industry wholesalers.

20. Attempt to sell to catalog houses.

21. Consider overseas markets.

22. Give sufficient attention to the library market.

23. Consider sales to government agencies.

24. Consider marketing similar books from other publishers.

25. Sell your book at every opportunity.

BUSINESS ORGANIZATION

26. Consult an attorney and a tax advisor to select the best business organization for you.

27. Choose a company name which conveys solidarity and reliability.

28. Plan to initially work out of your home.

29. Purchase general business insurance.

30. Check with state and local governments to obtain necessary business permits, licenses and identification numbers.

31. Obtain a post office box.

32. Install a commerical telephone line.

33. Keep backup copies of company records.

34. Arrange for another person to operate the business in your absence.

OFFICE EQUIPMENT

35. Purchase a powerful computer.

36. Consider purchasing a high quality printer for letters and a separate printer for preparing invoices, packing slips, etc. which require numerous copies.

37. Purchase other quality equipment including a copier, fax, typewriter, scale and phone answering system.

BUSINESS FORMS

38. Purchase letterheads, envelopes, invoices, packing slips, etc.

39. Make sure that a designated copy of the invoice can also be used as a packing slip.

40. Prepare a spacious order form for recording telephone orders.

LIBRARY OF CONGRESS CATALOG NUMBER

41. Request a Library of Congress Catalog Number in the year prior to publishing.

BOOK DESIGN

42. Plan to print a softcover book with perfect-binding.

43. Design an attractive cover realizing that colors are costly.

44. Make sure that your Library of Congress Catalog Number and properly worded copyright notice appear on the reverse side of the title page.

45. Make sure your book is at least 100 pages.

46. Prepare an index.

47. Apply for a Standard Account Number (SAN).

48. Obtain a UPC Bar Code Identification Number for printing on the back cover.

49. Obtain an ISBN Prefix Number for printing on the back cover.

PRINTERS

50. Plan to publish your book early in the year.

51. Seek price quotations and make sure that all printers are quoting on the same book size, covers, weight of paper, etc.

52. Obtain price quotations from at least three book manufacturers.

53. Be sure to consider transportation costs when comparing quotes.

54. Contact at least one distant printer located outside your state.

55. Order at least 2,500 to 3,000 copies.

56. Specify a high quality book.

57. Follow-up with your printer on the status of your order.

58. Upon receiving your books from the printer, verify that the quantity is correct.

59. Notify the printer immediately of any defects.

60. Purchase books in a carton size which can be reused for shipping large orders.

61. Apply for a copyright after book is printed.

FINANCIAL

62. Hire a good accounting firm.

63. Obtain separate bank checking and savings accounts.

64. Accept checks but not C.O.D.'s.

65. Deposit all incoming checks immediately.

66. Monitor your accounts receivables continuously.

67. Maintain an accurate list of slow paying and non-paying accounts.

68. Send notices to overdue accounts.

69. Pay all bills on time to build good credit.

70. Maintain a strict control of all expenses.

71. Keep receipts of all expenses.

72. Strive to build a cash reserve.

73. Keep payroll costs to an absolute minimum.

PRICING, TERMS AND CONDITIONS

74. Establish a retail book price which is at least six times the cost.

75. Attempt to set a retail book price under $10.00.

76. Establish bookseller's discounts.

77. Offer a 20% discount to public libraries.

78. Offer quantity discounts.

79. Require a one-half advance payment on large orders from new accounts.

80. Be sure your order form states "prices subject to change without notice."

81. State on order form that payment is to be in U.S. dollars.

82. Require purchase order numbers on sizeable orders from large companies and organizations.

83. Be sure to charge sales tax where applicable.

84. Establish shipping and handling charges which adequately cover your actual costs.

85. Prepare a returns policy requiring prior approval.

ADVERTISING AND SALES PROMOTION

86. Prepare a logo and company color scheme.

87. Prepare advertisements using short and powerful words with bold headings.

88. Make maximum use of the words "new" and "you."

89. Advertise in specialized publications aimed at your niche market.

90. Consider advertising in regional publications at a lower cost.

91. Experiment with direct mail.

92. Send direct mail to places of employment.

93. Make a special effort to receive a copy of all reviews.

94. Prepare promotional flyer sheets.

95. Maximize the use of reviews and testimonials.

96. Prepare a large order form for mailing with all shipments.

97. Maintain accurate sales records by customer for use in advertising-merchandising co-op programs.

PUBLICITY

98. Prepare a publicity release outlining a problem and explain how your book will solve it.

99. Prepare an announcement card for attaching to your complimentary review books.

100. Send complimentary book copies with a publicity release to book review editors at numerous magazines and newspapers.

101. List your book in all industry directories.

SHIPPING

102. Purchase a tape dispensing machine, cartons and plastic bubble wrap.

103. Inspect each book prior to shipping.

104. Enclose promotional literature and an order form with all shipments.

105. Include a thank you note with all shipments.

106. Mail an invoice with the book on shipments to individuals.

107. Package the book to ensure that it will arrive in perfect condition.

108. Use the Postal Service for small shipments and private carriers for larger shipments.

109. Ship all orders within 24–48 hours.

INVENTORY CONTROL

110. Store books in a dry location without major temperature changes.

111. Maintain accurate inventory records.

112. Keep an accurate record of sales by month and year to date.

113. Allow sufficient time for reordering books.

CUSTOMER SERVICE

114. Handle promptly all complaints, short shipments, etc.
115. Treat all customers equally and fairly.
116. Excel in customer service.

When It's Time to Actively Withdraw From the Business

A point will come in every publishing venture when it's time to quit active involvement. Age, poor health or "burn out" may have taken its toll.

You may simply get tired of making thousands of trips to the post office or bank. You may no longer want to rush an air shipment to a carrier's center after the driver has made the daily pick up.

Perhaps you are tired of writing new editions. The euphoria of finding your post office box filled with orders may now be replaced with thoughts of the work that will be required. The hassle of paying your bills while trying to collect from long overdue accounts may have gotten to you. You may have outgrown your facility and do not wish to make another major expenditure.

Fortunately, publishing is a business where you can withdraw from active involvement and continue to enjoy an income.

If you have a well established book with a strong sales record, you may wish to turn the publication over to a major publisher in return for royalties.

Publishers are obtained by sending query letters designed to stimulate interest. You can learn of the names of potential publishers by consulting various references at your library. Another approach is to visit a major bookstore and find out who is publishing similar books on your subject.

In order to impress a publisher, you will need to build a strong presentation for your book. Some of the elements that will influence a publisher are as follows:

> strong record of sales growth
> powerful reviews
> numerous editions and printings
> broad distribution by major wholesalers and book chains
> excellent profitability record
> popular subject with considerable growth potential

Once you receive a positive response from a query letter, you must sell yourself and the book. You need to emphasize your professional background and any qualifications that may add to the book's creditability such as education, lectures, awards, etc.

If preliminary discussions are favorable, you should consult an attorney who is experienced in publishing contracts. Many terms are subject to negotiations such as the amount of royalties and how they are to be determined.

If you can negotiate a fair contract, you may find yourself enjoying a great retirement and/or lifestyle while the royalties just roll in. What other business offers such a possibility?

INDEX